RELEASE THE DOVE

TIMELESS DEVOTIONAL

Rhonda Wilson-Dikoko

Table of Contents

About the Author 5

Acknowledgements 7

Dedication 9

Preface 10

Foreword | Anita Peeters 11

Day 1: Joy Cometh 14

Day 2: The Blood Will Never Lose Its Power 15

Day 3: ASH Wednesday 16

Day 4: The Power of Forgiveness 18

Day 5: Release Barabbas and let him go forever! 21

Testimony | Helena Moussounda 23

Day 6: Infinity Love 28

Day 7: The Healing Power of Jehovah Rapha 30

Day 8: Sweet Fragrances of the King 32

Day 9: A Sacrifice of Praise 35

Day 10: Released to do His Will 37

"Rising Free" 38

Day 11: Treasured, Talitha Koum Arise! Part I 39

Day 12: Treasured, Talitha Koum Arise! Part II 41

Day 13: The Power of Community 43

Day 14 - Being tempted is not the same as Falling into sin 45

Day 15 - Letting go of Fear of the Coronavirus I 46

Testimony | Carol Smart 49

Day 16 - Letting go of Fear to Praise the Lord II 54

Day 17 - Letting go of Fear, receive God's Insurance - His Protection Plan Part III 56

Day 18 - God Reveals His Plans to His Servants 59

Day 19 - Releasing the Kingdom of God upon the Earth 61

Day 20 - 2001 - The Year of my Consecration 65

Day 21 - A Sudden Halt! 67

Day 22 - Watch and Pray 69

Day 23- A National Day of Prayer 72

Day 24 - The Latter-Day Harvest is Ripe! 75

Day 25 - Sheep without a Shepherd 77

Testimony | Roxanne Cook 81

Day 26 - Shun Anxiousness, put on Gratefulness, be Thankful, wear Peace 88

Day 27 - Loose the Cords of Injustice 90

Day 28 - Spiritual Warfare/ Release Ungodly Thoughts 94

Day 29 - Be Prepared! 95

Day 30 - Emmanuel is with Us 98

Day 31 - Release Restoration over the Nations 103

Day 32 – Released from my Mind Prison!..................105

Day 33 – The Crown of Thorns......................108

Day 34 – The Branch..................................113

Testimony | Daria Morris..............................118

Day 35 – The Finest Hour of Christ's Glorious Church...........120

Day 36 – Those who Dream!...........................127

Day 37 – Spiritual Housecleaning.....................131

Day 38 – God's Great Commission – Release the Dove!.........135

Day 39 – The Lord is MY Shepherd – A Tribute to Rose.........138

Day 40 – Our Unchanging God.........................141

Editor's Note-Afterword | Katherine Voorvelt................145

Published by Rhonda Wilson-Dikoko
Publishing partner: Paragon Publishing, Rothersthorpe

© Rhonda Wilson-Dikoko 2020

The rights of Rhonda Wilson-Dikoko to be identified as the author of this work have been asserted by her in accordance with the Copyright, Designs and Patents Act of 1988.
All rights reserved; no part of this publication may be reproduced, stored in a retrieval system, or transmitted in any form or by any means, electronic, mechanical, photocopying, recording or otherwise without the prior written consent of the publisher or a licence permitting copying in the UK issued by the Copyright Licensing Agency Ltd.
www.cla.co.uk

ISBN 978-1-78222-761-8

Book design, layout and production management by Into Print
www.intoprint.net
+44 (0)1604 832149

About the Author

Rhonda Wilson-Dikoko was born in Fayette, Alabama on February 3, 1964. Her Father urged her to study nursing after High School, so she did. But her real passion was journalism. She dabbled in it during High School and later took courses in Creative Writing.

Rhonda married Clement Dikoko from Congo, Africa, in 1986 and moved to Congo in 1988. Rhonda considers herself a Global Citizen. She and her husband, now both ministers, have lived in many different countries, on 4 continents doing ministry wherever they go. They have 3 children Alesea, twins Obiale and Danielle, a son in law Carmelo and two grand-children Olivier and Sanaa.

Rhonda's Ministry has spanned over 30 years with an emphasis on Women Ministry and under-privileged children. Rhonda hails from Double Portion Church where she was ordained in 2001 under the auspices of Pastor Hayse Moss and Evangelist Sarah Banks. Rhonda is fluent in French and traveled for many years with Sis Sarah (as many fondly call her) as her personal interpreter. Rhonda was the Bible Study Leader for Oasis in Malaysia for 6 years. She loves to empower women and help stir up their passion for Jesus as well as discover their giftings. Her vision was for Oasis members from their various walks of life to start up Oasis Satellites wherever they go. That is already coming into fruition. Rhonda was Director of an Orphanage in Pointe Noire, Congo and helped to fund raise for that orphanage and many other outreaches and causes she might have stumbled upon during her travels.

Rhonda has been writing "The Sacred Words of a Sage Femme" to be released at the Lord's bidding. She and her husband currently reside in Texas, USA.

Photography by Shuhada Hasim

Acknowledgements

I would like to thank Katherine Voorvelt, my very dear and sacred friend for her invaluable help to painstakingly edit these devotions. Her re-verifying and clarifying my words have no doubt improved the fluidity for your reading pleasure.

I am honored to receive a beautiful endorsement from Mary Thomas through her words of affirmation. Mary Thomas is a Covenant Sister Partner, a friend who sticks closer than a 'a brother'.

I will forever cherish the friendship of my Agape sister, Anita Peeters, a "true sister from another mother". Thank you, Anita, for your inviting me to be a part of such a wonderful praying group of sisters. Having Agape meals in your warm home on a cold winter's day in The Hague was such joy. Always surrounded by beauty in every corner, paintings done by your Soulmate that I envision one day will be in an exhibition, served to transport me to that secret place in His presence.

Your validation of who I am, by single handedly pushing your own campaign, buying copies of my books, and giving them to people who needed them, supporting me on every whim has been a blessing. Thank you, dear friend, for your foreword which serves as an appetizer to launch the reader into this devotional which I hope and pray, will be an immense blessing to them daily.

I am infinitely grateful to my 'baby girl' Danielle for once more using her polished skills to put this devotional together from front to back in the format it is today.

Finally, I would like to thank my husband Clement, for his calm, quiet reserve, providing space for me to write at my leisure. Thank you for our evening walks in the cool of the day, your magnificent photography captured on many pages for the reader's pleasure. You should consider doing photography as a hobby. Thanks for giving me 35 years of marital bliss!

May I introduce my family to you: Left to right: Twins Danielle and her brother Clement Jr, son-in-law Mel, daughter Alesea, husband Clement, and grand-children, Sanaa and Olivier.

Dedication

Rock of Ages, Lover of my Soul, Way Maker, Healer, Mighty Deliverer, Food to the Hungry, Drink for the Thirsty, Confidant, Miracle Worker, Lord of Lord and King of Kings, I worship you! If not for your guidance and miracles in my life I would never have been able to pen them on these pages.

You are the TRUE author and FINISHER of my faith. My footsteps are ordered by you. When I set out to write this Devotional in Holland, France, Jerusalem, Italy, and Tunisia you knew it was not meant to be. Your plans are always the best. Though I did not have the experience of writing from those wonderfully spiritual and ancient destinations, not once did you NOT give me inspiration or provide me with fresh manna for the day, thank you Abba.

I am so grateful to the Oasis Bible Study of Houston for taking part of the Release the Dove Study. Thanks to Chelsa Russell, who helped me set up a platform on Facebook to post daily.

I am honored to the Release Community who devoured my posts, responded with gratitude, and encouraged me daily by their reflections.

A big kudos, merci, gracias, dank u, Terima Kasih, Spasibo to those searching souls who obtained a copy of this book for your 40-day journey. May your 40 days be as sweet as ours, the Release Community. We were immensely blessed during the time of "famine and plague" in the 'world' yet in "Goshen" we received daily the blessings of the Lord that 'maketh rich and addeth no sorrow'. May you also experience this tremendous benediction for you and your loved ones during your sojourn.

Preface

Release the Dove Devotional was planned to be a timeless devotional to be used during any season of one's life.

During my grandson's illness which I write about in Release the Dove Book, I had gone on a 'Word Fast' during the Lent season. I wanted to 'fast my words' as well as hear God's. I so desired to be immersed in a continual overflow of dialog with the Father and that is exactly what I experienced! He spoke to me through scripture, His Living Word, through objects, to my heart and sometimes I perceived that I even heard an audible voice.

My relationship with The Father during that season was so tender and special I did not dare leave his presence. I did not want to miss one Word, one thought, one occasion to hear His Voice. No language to me was as important as the Language of the Holy Spirit and hearing from God. Long after the Fast was over, my grandson was healed and had returned to the USA with his Mom, I still found myself groping for Words, until this day actually. I became as one who was mute, my conversation was The Word and my communication was with God.

The Finger of God impressed upon my heart to write the Release book and workbook. I desired to write a devotional however circumstances in my life kept me from doing so till now. I have taken a Sabbatical during the Lent Season 2020 once more to hear from God. My heart's cry is that you may glean a word, an experience, a scripture and take hold Beloved, for this is *YOUR* time to receive from the Father's heart.

In His Service, Rhonda

Foreword | Anita Peeters

Pastor Rhonda is one of those souls whose depth of faith in God will leave you wanting to know more of Him. She greatly encourages others with her love of Jesus, sharing with passion and vigour. Her resilient faith has been wrought over many years, through travelling along the high roads and the valleys, allowing her to share to a wider audience with credibility and conviction.

I have had the honour of walking with Rhonda for several years and can testify to her rich and broad testimonies which she uses to point others to Jesus. Having lived in a variety of countries, she well understands the many complex differences and is able to seamlessly bring together people of all backgrounds and deliver a fresh message which resonates across cultural divides.

I can personally attest to her devotion for our small group of believers here in The Hague, our Agape Sisters, as we set out on a fast together seeking His will for our lives in the area of family restoration. As we started our fast, she shared her unique and stimulating perspective into our daily readings, always ready with an encouraging verse, a well-thought insight or a different angle on a familiar Bible story or a prophecy specifically for each one of us. She encouraged us to ensure that the Holy Spirit was central to our steps forward, and her spirit-led prayers (which once included blowing the shofar!) often led us into spontaneous praise and worship. During our fast, our small band of sisters saw personal breakthroughs and such incredible answers to prayer, the impacts of which are still being outworked in our lives today.

Her Release the Dove daily devotional contains many insights into her personal revelation of God's love for her, as well as in the lives of others around her. She carries His Word high and is diligent and purposeful in shining His light into dark places, encouraging others to taste real freedom and deliverance. She infuses joy in her words and her enthusiasm is palpable as she seeks to connect people to the good news of the gospel.

Throughout her devotional, she weaves a thread to show how God always leads His people and stands true on His promises. This is also true in her own life and through her own unique experiences, she is able to easily share her testimony and encourage others to believe that what God can do for the one, He will also do for many. Her words will lift you up, encourage you to shift your gaze back to Jesus, remind you that He has a purpose and plan for your life, and will gently lead you to dwell in the secret places and to seek His Word.

Her knowledge and understanding of the Word is clear, and her teaching of it is salient and sure. Her personal perspective of God as Heavenly Father, carrier of our cares and sure anchor of our hope in a wave-tossed world, is a breath of life in all seasons. She draws from her own experiences to remind us that He is always true to His Word, He sustains us with His hope, He is Healer and Redeemer, and throughout our lives, He provides us with a song in the night and His mercies are new every morning.

I know for certain that this devotional is going to be a great blessing for many, especially during this current season, and that through her words God has already strategically sown seed which will reap a harvest so great, the ripple effect which may not be known this side of heaven but that the angels are already rejoicing.

- - - -

Anita Peeters is passionate about Jesus and has had the honour to share His good news from Sydney to the Solomon Islands, Berlin to The Hague. She loves connecting with women from all walks of life and encouraging them to reach their potential, know God in a personal way and experience His freedom in their life. She also loves the outdoors and taking long bike rides in the Dutch countryside.

Day 1: Joy Cometh

"For his anger lasts only a moment, but his favor lasts a lifetime; weeping may stay for the night but rejoicing comes in the morning." **Psalms 30:5 (NIV)**

I had spent a year lamenting in a state of perpetual depression and oppression brought on by my own hand. I had thought at some point I would die in my sleep because of it all. I was mournful and sorrowful but reluctant to give this state of being up to the Father. It was as if I could save myself from this calamity. I had been so saddened and disappointed in myself that I would not allow the Savior to rescue me. I could barely hear his voice anymore because of a callous heart. I had foolishly allowed deceit to seep in.

Then joy came wrapped up in a bundle of love called Olivier. I was given the awesome honor to name our grandson and with careful contemplation I did so. I had vowed not to take him in while his Mom and Dad were completing University, I wanted them to feel the weight of the responsibility of raising their son upon their shoulders. However, by the time Olivier reached 11 ½ months, he was taking flights across the great Atlantic to live with KoKo and Grandpa!

When you realize and fully accept that the GREAT I AM is the one who has eradicated our sins and sits at the right hand of the Father interceding on your behalf, you graciously learn to accept the Olive Branch of Grace extended to you. You quickly accept that the blood shed upon Calvary NEVER loses its power. For it is by grace you have been saved, through faith--and this is not from yourselves, it is the gift of God, **Ephesians 2.8 (NIV).**

Pray: *Lord I accept graciously your gift of salvation. I release depression, oppression and refuse to continue to weep when you* *have sent your JOY announced by the angels to the shepherds in* **Luke 2:10 NASB** *"But the angel said to them, 'Do not be afraid! For behold, I bring you good news of great joy that will be for all the people: 11 Today in the City of David a Savior has been born to you. He is Christ the Lord!'." Joy Cometh, I embrace it! I wear it! I receive it! In Jesus Name Amen.*

Day 2: The Blood Will Never Lose Its Power

The Blood Releases me from all my fears!

This old hymn, "The Blood will never lose its Power" is one that touches you deep down in your soul. Today's devotional will be active in that you are required to spend a few moments downloading this song from YouTube, listening and meditating on its words. As you do so, Release the fears that have kept you bound paralyzing you from going forth in your Purpose!

The Blood never loses its power
The blood that Jesus shed for me,
way back on Calvary;
the blood that gives me strength
from day to day,
it will never lose its power.

Chorus:
It reaches to the highest mountain,
and it flows to the lowest valley;
the blood that gives me strength
from day to day,
it will never lose its power.

Verse 2:
It soothes my doubts and calms my fears,
and it dries all my tears;
the blood that gives me strength
from day to day,
it will never lose its power.

Pray:
Father, I acknowledge that your blood shed for me on Calvary is enough to cleanse me from all iniquity. I ask Father O Lord from the top of my head to the bottom of my feet, that you would cleanse me today in Jesus Mighty Name. I actively release every fear plaguing me today (name them) In Jesus Mighty Name Amen.

Day 3: ASH Wednesday

I attended my first ASH Wednesday Service this week at The Woodlands Church. I was excited but curious to go as this would serve also as the commencement of our 40-Day Devotional and Fast. I learned that Ash Wednesday symbolizes the Christian belief that humans were created from dust and will return to dust and ash when they die. This belief, however, is offset by the belief that the death of Christ allowed for people to be more than simply dust; it allowed for an eternal life in heaven, outside the body.

This practice and tradition were a revelation to me but not the belief. Our Christian walk has been beautifully shaped with the knowledge of an eternal life with the Father. Just knowing that Jesus has conquered death and we will pass from life on earth to life in eternity is a comforting thought for all who know the Lord! But where we spend eternity must be decided upon whilst we still have breath in our lungs. Repenting from our sins and embracing Jehovah

Tsidkenu, God our Righteousness, is key in understanding the Salvation Jesus has wrought for our sins! Thank God for Ash Wednesday and Thank God for Jesus and the Cross!

As we discussed at Oasis Bible Study on Tuesday prior to beginning this Devotional and Fast, I felt that there were many novices entering into these 40 days with some trepidation. The thought of giving up something we treasure for 40 days can be a bit frustrating as the flesh desires all that is contrary to the Spirit. I tried to console our sisters by emphasizing that the focus should not be on what you are giving up rather what you will gain.

Galatians 5:17 (NIV) says the following:
"For the flesh desires what is contrary to the Spirit, and the Spirit what is contrary to the flesh. They are in conflict with each other, so that you are not to do whatever you want."

Paul says it better in **Romans 7:21-24 (NIV)**:
"**21** So I find this law at work: Although I want to do good, evil is right there with me. **22** For in my inner being I delight in God's law; 23 but I see another law at work in me, waging war against the law of my mind and making me a prisoner of the law of sin at work within me. **24** What a wretched man I am! Who will rescue me from this body that is subject to death? **25** Thanks be to God, who delivers me through Jesus Christ our Lord! So then, I myself in my mind am a slave to God's law, but in my sinful nature[d] a slave to the law of sin."

Pray:
Dear Father, just the knowledge of knowing that our body will not remain ashes, but you will reconstitute it at the proper time according to your sacred Word in **1 Corinthians 15:53** *is enough just to give me complete peace in the concept of the resurrection of the dead. It also allows me to enter into this 40-day devotional denying*

my fleshly body earthly food whilst I feed my spirit man, spiritual food. Thank you, Lord, for changing my perspective, in Jesus Name, Amen.

Day 4: The Power of Forgiveness

David stood in the backyard gazing up at John David's tree he had planted only a few years back. David had planted an oak tree for every member of his family. He allowed his thoughts to take him back to the day he purchased the trees, bought fish as fertilizer and watched his children water their tender shoots. John David the eldest of the two used to fight with his sister Suzanne over whose tree was the tallest. Today his tree stood almost the same height as the other three. But John David would never see his tree grow up, he would never graduate from High School or go to college. His tender young life had been snatched away in a freak gun accident.

David sobbed softly to himself as the guests mingled in his home talking quietly amongst themselves in hope of bringing comfort to his family by their presence. But David wanted none of it. He preferred standing in the backyard in the rain to being cramped up in the house with a bunch of folks who understood nothing of his family's pain and turmoil brought on by the loss of their son.

For the first time in his life, David felt utterly helpless and alone, unable to do anything to remedy the situation. He felt doomed to a life of despair and hopelessness. "Senseless!" David muttered under his voice. Intense anger taking hold of his entire being. The death of his son did not make any sense to him. How could a loving God be so cruel?

He didn't want to go back into the house with the crowd, he preferred to be outside alone in the cold winter temperature rather than enjoy the warmth of the hearth and company inside. David looked intensely at his deceased child's tree startled to find a dove peering back at him! Normally doves would take flight at the mildest of noise but not this dove. He sat perched in John David's tree staring straight at him!

David took a step towards the tree, but the dove didn't even flinch. David kept vigil each day watching the tree until one day he discovered there was a nest with 2 eggs! Somehow this sign brought great comfort to him as he believed in his heart John David was with the Lord. He also felt the two eggs meant God would bless him with two more children, and He did! David and his wife Jody had two more sons!

One of those sons, Brian grew up to become a lawyer. He had grown up hearing about his brother's death and wanted to do research on the boy who had shot him. He knew a monument had been erected at John David's school in memory of his life but what of the young man who had taken his brother's life?

What Brian discovered was not surprising. The young man had had a turbulent childhood drifting in and out of trouble. He later married and had children but seemed to barely be surviving in life. Brian felt for this young man and told his Father he believed strongly in the power of forgiveness. He told his Dad he should visit the shooter and release him from the debt of murder that must surely be weighing him down.

A year had gone by since David had been told this by his youngest son Brian, yet he had taken nary a step towards restitution of the killer's own life. Thirty years had gone by since his son's death and David and his family had lived successful lives. He felt like he had forgiven the young man who terminated his son's life but had not properly released him. Now he was ready to do so. He planned to gather his family, even bring his daughter from Seattle and go to visit the young man. He asked me to pray for him and his family.

Forgiveness can lead to feelings of understanding, empathy and compassion for the one who hurt you. Forgiveness doesn't mean forgetting or excusing the harm done to you or making up with the person who caused the harm. Forgiveness brings a kind of peace that helps you go on with life in addition to releasing the guilty person(s).

Holding on to unforgiveness is a blessing blocker in your life. Look at what Jesus says in **Matthew 18:18-22 (NIV): 19** "Again, truly I tell you that if two of you on earth agree about anything they ask for, it will be done for them by my Father in heaven. **20** For where two or three gather in my name, there am I with them." **21** Then Peter came to Jesus and asked, "Lord, how many times shall I forgive my brother or sister who sins against me? Up to seven times?" **22** Jesus answered, "I tell you, not seven times, but seventy-seven times."
In Verse **19** Jesus tells us how to get our prayers answered. In the next breath he reiterates the exact same thing letting us know that we should extend unlimited grace to those who wrong us because we ourselves have been recipients of the grace of God.

In the Bible, the Greek word translated "forgiveness" literally means "to let go," as when a person does not demand payment for a debt. Jesus used this comparison when he taught his followers to pray: "And forgive us our sins, for we also forgive everyone who is indebted to us." **Luke 11:4 (NIV).**

Pray: *Lord Forgive me of my sins and I also forgive and release _____ for doing wrong to me. Today, I choose to forgive and to let go, in Jesus Mighty Name Amen. David and his family's story was shared with his express permission in the hopes of helping others get* through their pain. His eldest daughter Suzanne lives in Seattle with her husband and their son. Christopher and Brian live in the Clear Lake area near their parents. Please continue to pray for his family.

Side Note: The process of forgiveness may entail more in-depth prayers depending on your circumstance, please feel free to write to me privately if you need additional assistance in the process of forgiveness.

Day 5: Release Barabbas and let him go forever!

A group of us gathered in my living-room to watch a smuggled copy of The Passion of the Christ. My husband and I were living in a compound in Nigeria at the time. My urgency and desire to spread the gospel to my neighbors and friends outweighed the guilt of procuring a boot-legged copy of the movie.

It was during the Easter Season yet many in my sphere of influence knew nothing of the Lord. So, I invited some of my friends and neighbors to watch a 'film at home'. I had popcorn and drinks but from the offset of the movie, it was difficult to enjoy a morsel of food or even a drink. My unsaved friends were undone. Some even cried to see the brutal assault on an innocent man.

When one is guilty, human nature has the tendency to accept a certain belief that one should be punished. But what if one is innocent as in the case of our Savior Jesus Christ, the One and Only? It was totally inhuman and unimaginable to fathom such a cruel, heartless death perpetrated by his own people.

Let's read the account of his trial from **Luke 23:13-24 (NIV):**
"**13** Pilate called together the chief priests, the rulers and the people,

14 and said to them, 'You brought me this man as one who was inciting the people to rebellion. I have examined him in your presence and have found no basis for your charges against him. **15** Neither has Herod, for he sent him back to us; as you can see, he has done nothing to deserve death. **16** Therefore, I will punish him and then release him.' **[17] [a]**
18 But the whole crowd shouted 'Away with this man! Release Barabbas to us!' **19** (Barabbas had been thrown into prison for an insurrection in the city, and for murder.)
20 Wanting to release Jesus, Pilate appealed to them again. **21** But they kept shouting, 'Crucify him! Crucify him!' **22** For the third time he spoke to them: 'Why? What crime has this man committed? I have found in him no grounds for the death penalty. Therefore, I will have him punished and then release him.' **23** But with loud shouts they insistently demanded that he be crucified, and their shouts prevailed. **24** So Pilate decided to grant their demand. **25** He released the man who had been thrown into prison for insurrection and murder, the one they asked for, and surrendered Jesus to their will."

In the case of Christ, we observe the brutal murder of an innocent man. **Isaiah 53** paints a picture of his crucifixion that Mel Gibson chose to portray in The Passion of The Christ using the 4 gospels as his source of material. Yet while Jesus was still on the cross, he prayed this prayer on behalf of his murderers:
Luke 23:34 (NIV) : "Jesus said, 'Father, forgive them, for they do not know what they are doing.' And they divided up his clothes by casting lots."

How many of you have been falsely accused in your life and wanted to get revenge? All of us at one time in our lives I'm sure have screamed bloody murderer at our accusers. We have dreamed, plotted and consoled ourselves just with the thought of sweet revenge. But not Jesus Christ. He prayed for those who persecuted him. As Christians, we should imitate his actions and do the same.

Who do you need to forgive today? Who has falsely accused you and you are counting the days till they will be destroyed or struck down by lightning or even worst! Are you ready to let that go and release it to God? Let us pray.

Pray: *Dear heavenly Father, I have been falsely accused and this has hurt me to the core, causing me sleepless nights and a desire for revenge. But today I have read of your own account and how you so eloquently responded to the insults of your accusers.*

Father, I want to be like you. I want to release "Barabbas" the insurrectionist in my life. He has done great harm to me, but I choose to forgive and to release him into your capable hands. He deserves to suffer, he deserves to feel the same pain he inflicted on me but Oh Lord, with your help, I release him today, in Jesus mighty Name I pray, Amen and Amen.

Thank you, Father, for helping me to do this difficult task.

Reflections

_____

_____

_____

_____

_____

_____

Testimony | Helena Moussounda

My husband and I were living a dream life. He had been promoted to a very superior level in his company but unfortunately experienced a burnt out that led him to the decision to resign. When he made that decision, all the pressure and burdens he previously felt seamlessly disappeared. He felt in his spirit, we needed to return to the USA. Initially, I was disappointed as I loved living overseas, but I quickly made all the arrangements to return to the USA. I was able to place my son's nanny in a good home making a good income, that was important to me. We chose to leave our oldest son with friends so he could complete his 12th grade year.

Before returning to the USA, two things happened that made us realize our footsteps had been ordered by the Lord. Six days after my husband made the decision to resign, we received our green cards for residency in the USA! We were already Canadian citizens but now God had doubly blessed us with this wonderful gift!

The second thing that occurred was the Covid19 which swept the world by storm. Most of my friends felt that I must have been lucky for leaving JUST IN TIME. My husband and I made the decision to have our son join us in the USA. Many had to be evacuated. I told them it was not luck but providence. God had ordered our footsteps and worked out everything for our good! We are ever so grateful! The LORD directs the steps of the godly. He delights in every detail of their lives. **Psalms 37:23 NLT**. And we know that God causes everything to work together for the good of those who love God and are called according to his purpose for them, Romans 8:28 NLT.

Reflections

You will keep *Him* in perfect peace, Whose mind is stayed on *You*, Because he trusts in You.

Isaiah 26:3 KJV

Day 6: Infinity Love

So tiny and so precious and beautiful is he,
Who would ever believe that this angel was sent to me?
You came much too soon, we were totally caught by surprise,
Yet when you appeared in our world on August 3rd,
All the pain and fears we had, begun to subside.

I love you more than anything and I will always pray,
That the Lord would grant you peace and in His perfect will you would stay. I pray that the Lord would guide and protect you,
And keep you through the storms of life ---
Help you when you stumble
Keep you away from strife.

So just how much do you love me Koko?
I'm sure one day you may ask.
Infinity x2
Forever and always will be my reply!

I wrote this poem on Aug 3, 2005 when Olivier was born, he has always called me Koko. (Koko means Grandma in Lingala, my husband's native language). I had been standing in the Labor Room praying for Olivier to come into this world and anticipating the joy his life would bring. Alesea was weary, I was tired. Alesea had wanted to deliver drug-free but the wait had been too long and the pain too great! The Psalmist said: "In my desperation I prayed, and the Lord listened; He saved me from all my troubles." **Psalm 34:6 (NLT)** Save us Lord Jesus I cried!

 TD Jakes had a "Woman Thou Art Loosed" Conference in Atlanta I was scheduled to be at the next day. Friends were coming from Gabon, Africa to join me at this event. We are waiting and anticipating. Mel paces the floor, wrings his hands, not knowing what to do to alleviate Alesea's pain.

"I'm going for chicken wings at Walmart next door," I said, needing to get out of that space into the fresh air.

Walking to my car, I lifted my hands towards the heavens and called upon the name of the Lord to intervene.

Arriving back at the hospital, things have accelerated, and Life is about to happen!

Thank you, Lord, "Weeping may last but for the night, but a shout of joy comes in the morning!" **Psalms 30:5b (NASB).**

That Labor Room experience taught me how to PUSH (Pray until something happens) in prayer when life gets tough!

You might be going through a 'labor room' experience at this very moment. The expected outcome just hasn't happened as planned. Obstacles are in the way and you just want to throw in the towel. The pain is too severe, and you simply want to give up, bail out and let that baby go!
I'd like to encourage you today NOT to give up instead PUSH!

Pray: *Lord, I'm tired, weary and worn. I don't know which way to turn. Your Word says that weeping lasts for a night, but joy comes in the morning. I've wept too long Lord! I'm ready for your joy to appear! I'm ready for my 'morning' to come! In Jesus Name I have prayed, Amen!*

I promise you if you pray that prayer with all sincerity, continue to PUSH in the Spirit, God will move on your behalf! I'm joining you in prayer!

Day 7: The Healing Power of Jehovah Rapha

A friend of mine came to visit and as she left, I wanted to leave her with a benediction that I'll now share with you.

Healing is the Greek word "Idamai", which means to cure, to restore or to heal. Jehovah- Rapha, the Balm in Gilead, heals and delivers mankind of spiritual, emotional and physical encumbrances! And He sometimes uses YOU to accomplish this!

Look at these scriptures below:

Acts 5:15 (NIV):
"As a result, people brought the sick into the streets and laid them on beds and mats so that at least Peter's shadow might fall on some of them as he passed by."

Acts 19:12 (NIV):
"so that even handkerchiefs and aprons that had touched him were taken to the sick, and their illnesses were cured, and the evil spirits left them." (Speaking of Paul).

2 Kings 13:21 (NIV):
"Once while some Israelites were burying a man, suddenly they saw a band of raiders; so, they threw the man's body into Elisha's tomb. When the body touched Elisha's bones, the man came to life and stood up on his feet."

Mark 16:17-18 (KJV):
"17 And these signs shall follow them that believe; In my name shall they cast out devils; they shall speak with new tongues.
18 They shall take up serpents; and if they drink any deadly thing, it

shall not hurt them; they shall lay hands on the sick, and they shall recover."

These are all powerful scriptures that teach us Jesus Heals! He uses the foolish things to confound the wise! **1 Corinthians 1:27**

An apron, a handkerchief, a shadow and our hands. But what's the common denominator? Yes, Jesus was in each of these situations as part of the Trinity. The Holy Spirit was present and working with them.

Acts 10:38 (NIV):
"how God anointed Jesus of Nazareth with the Holy Spirit and power, and how he went around doing good and healing all who were under the power of the devil, because God was with him."

The Great Commission was given to us as believers. We need to go into all the world and preach the gospel. In today's age, many have begun to preach via television, YouTube and many GO as missionaries to various countries and devote their lives to this kind of work. But often, the Lord simply uses us in our current circumstances to be light and salt to others around us in our sphere of influence. He has given us the Great Commission as our commissioning Papers, and He's promised to be with us. In addition, he's given us the Holy Spirit! What more could we ask for?

Matthew 28:16-20 (NIV):
"The Great Commission
16 Then the eleven disciples went to Galilee, to the mountain where Jesus had told them to go. **17** When they saw him, they worshiped him; but some doubted. **18** Then Jesus came to them and said, 'All authority in heaven and on earth has been given to me. **19** Therefore go and make disciples of all nations, baptizing them in the name of the Father and of the Son and of the Holy Spirit, **20** and teaching

them to obey everything I have commanded you. And surely, I am with you always, to the very end of the age.'" Hallelujah. Emmanuel promises to be with us throughout it all. What an assurance! What a peace of mind! Leaning on the everlasting arms of Christ.

Let us pray:
"Heavenly Father, our faith remains rooted and grounded in your Word, not just historical things and events. Although it is integrally related to life we pray that our own faith may grow strong and be powerful as we see the despair around us, the shaking of foundations, the changing of that which has long been taken to be permanent, the overthrowing of empires and the rising of others.

Abba, our eyes are steadfast on you as our Unchanging Omnipresent God. The One Whose Word is Eternal. As the Lord Jesus himself said, "Heaven and earth shall pass away, but my Word shall never pass away." **Matthew 24:35 (KJV)** *(Lift up your hands as a sign of surrender unto God). Use me, oh Lord in this latter day to become a catalyst for change. In my sphere of influence, enable me to Release the Dove and see miraculous occurrences take place. I pray in Jesus Mighty name, Amen.*

If you prayed that prayer with a sincere heart, get ready for a supernatural manifestation to take place!

Day 8: Sweet Fragrances of the King

Last night our Oasis group met for the last time during this season. It is primarily for them that I commenced this 40-day devotional journey we are on as an extension of our meetings.

Last night we worshipped listening to Alabaster Box by CeCe Winans. If you've never heard this beautiful song, I would encourage you to do so. It is about Mary who broke an expensive bottle of pure nard perfume and washed the feet of Jesus. You see, I wanted us to complete our study by giving God the praise He is worthy of. God exceeded our expectations on many of our prayer requests and is still at work in our lives to finish what He started. Won't you give Him some praise right now?

I wrote this timeless exhortation in 2011 during the Christmas season however it is still pertinent for us today. What kind of aromas and fragrance tantalize your senses during the Christmas season? In some homes, there may be the aroma of fresh cut Christmas pine trees, others may have the fragrance of spices from baked pecan pies or ginger from delectable gingerbread cookies.

For my husband's 50th, I chose to buy one of the most expensive colognes ever made from Amouage. I was blessed to get it from the 'source' of where it is manufactured in Oman in the Middle East. This cologne's fragrance is called Gold. Clement brought it to the USA with intentions of saving it for his retirement! Our son recently discovered it in his closet and playfully pretended to steal it! If you know these two personally, you know they are jokesters!

The Bible speaks of Mary in **John 12:3** who took about a pint of pure nard, an expensive perfume which was imported from northern India (Brown 19966:448); she poured it on Jesus' feet and wiped his feet with her hair as an act of worship. The cost was indicative of her praise for the Master! The house was filled with the fragrance of the perfume.

Both aspects of her action--the extravagance and the method--were disturbing. Judas says, no doubt correctly, that it was worth a year's wages (**John 12:5**). The text literally reads "three hundred denarii" (cf. NIV note). Since a denarius was a day's pay for a day laborer, the NIV paraphrase is accurate, considering feast days and Sabbaths when one would not work. A rough equivalent would be something over $10,000, the gross pay for someone working at minimum wage for a year. No wonder the disciple, Judas, responded with dismay at such a waste (**Matthew 26:8 (NIV)**).

There is a fragrance that each one of us carry when we walk into a room. We can enhance the atmosphere in which we inhabit, or we can render the environment toxic with our negativity, our complaints, and our bad moods.

When our twins were in their teens experiencing the realities of that time, their personalities were as different as they come. One was often moody and the other upbeat and exuberant. I used to lecture them about the importance of their fragrance, their perfume, how they affect the world in which they live, for no one is an island.

Mary's perfume so affected the life of everyone in that house that day including Judas, who betrayed Jesus, all the other disciples there as well as the Pharisees. You don't need to buy the $10,000 pure nard that Mary used to wash Jesus feet or even the Amouage Gold which I purchased for Clément's 50th birthday. Just make up your mind to be a sweet aroma that contaminates the world and the ones around you. Just decide that you will practice being the hands and feet of Jesus in the world you live in by reaching out to others.

Let us use this scripture as our prayer focus today. You may personalize it:

2 Corinthians 2:14-17 (NIV) says this:
"**14** But thanks be to God, who always leads us as captives in Christ's triumphal procession and uses us to spread the aroma of the knowledge of him everywhere. **15** For we are to God the pleasing

aroma of Christ among those who are being saved and those who are perishing. **16** To the one we are an aroma that brings death; to the other, an aroma that brings life. And who is equal to such a task? 17 Unlike so many, we do not peddle the word of God for profit. On the contrary, in Christ we speak before God with sincerity, as those sent from God."

Dearly Beloved, let our fragrance contaminate all around us by spreading peace, love and joy to all you meet. Now that is priceless!

Day 9: A Sacrifice of Praise

In continuation of our worship, I wanted to share a passage of scripture that has meant a lot to me over the years.

Psalm 103:1-5 (NKJV):
1 "Bless the Lord, O my soul,
and all that is within me,
bless his holy name!
2 Bless the Lord, O my soul,
and forget not all his benefits,
3 who forgives all your iniquities,
who heals all your diseases,
4 who redeems your life from destruction,
who crowns you with loving kindness and tender mercies,
5 who satisfies your mouth with good things,
so that your youth is renewed like the eagle's."

How many times have we gone to Church and just didn't feel like giving God any praise? I remember in Congo when I was going through a particularly rough stretch, I would dance before God with all my might during every praise and worship service. A Pastor's wife came up to me on one of these occasions and told me she just did NOT understand my praise! When I should be grumbling and complaining, I choose to praise!

There are times that we can offer up a sacrifice of praise. We can remember that we are still breathing and that simply is a gift from God. We can remember that we praise God for who he is despite whatever circumstances you might be in.

The word "sacrifice" (Greek, "thusia") comes from the root "thuo", a verb meaning "to kill or slaughter for a purpose." Praise often requires that we "kill" our pride or fear—that we release our addictions, anything we deem in our lives as being ungodly. Habits that threaten to diminish or interfere with our worship of the Lord.

What do you need to kill or slaughter in your life that is keeping you from giving God all the glory? Is it an addiction, a love of food or drug of your choice? Do you have an idol such as television or sports, or does your husband, wife, child (ren) prohibit you from worshipping the Lord wholeheartedly? Virtually anything that you exalt over God becomes an idol.

Did you know that you could even have a sickness or illness that hinders your praise? That is why the Psalmist David spoke to his Soul and commanded it to Bless the Lord! We sometimes need to sacrifice these things on the altar in order to fully praise the Lord.

Prayer:
I willingly sacrifice _____ to praise you during this 40-day fast and beyond. Lord deliver me from _____ so that I can be completely totally free to worship you. Thank you, Lord Jesus.
1 "Bless the Lord, O my soul,
and all that is within me,
bless his holy name!

*2 Bless the Lord, O my soul,
and forget not all his benefits,
3 who forgives all your iniquities,
who heals all your diseases,
4 who redeems your life from destruction,
who crowns you with loving kindness and tender mercies,
5 who satisfies your mouth with good things,
so that your youth is renewed like the eagles."
Hallelujah! Praise God! Amen and Amen!*

Day 10: Released to do His Will

Hebrews 10:4-10 (NIV) :
"**4** It is impossible for the blood of bulls and goats to take away sins. **5** Therefore, when Christ came into the world, he said:
'Sacrifice and offering you did not desire,
but a body you prepared for me;
6 with burnt offerings and sin offerings
you were not pleased.
7 Then I said, 'Here I am—it is written about me in the scroll—
I have come to do your will, my God.'"
8 First he said, "Sacrifices and offerings, burnt offerings and sin offerings you did not desire, nor were you pleased with them"—though they were offered in accordance with the law. **9** Then he said, "Here I am, I have come to do your will." He sets aside the first to establish the second. **10** And by that will, we have been made holy through the sacrifice of the body of Jesus Christ once for all."

Pray:
Father, only your blood can cleanse me so that I may do your will. Prepare my heart, I exchange today, your will for mine. In Jesus Mighty Name, Amen.

"Rising Free"

Dave Voorvelt, the artist who painted 'Rising Free', was Katherine Voorvelt's beloved husband for many years before he passed 3 years ago. He had a deep understanding of the plight of women in many societies and greatly admired the strength of women evidenced in the various African countries he lived or worked in and also when they moved to The Netherlands to live.

The inspiration for 'Rising Free' came from the women living in the towns and fishing villages along the banks of Lake Nyasa in Malawi. See how the water birds on the 'Chitengi' wrap fabric come alive and rise up and fly free. The three doves are held gently in the loving hands of the two women just before being released. There is a strength evident in the women indicating resolution, determination, and purpose.

Day 11: Treasured, Talitha Koum Arise! Part I

I arrived in my beloved second home, The Netherlands this morning. If you have traveled overseas you realize what the time difference can do to someone's body (roughly 7 hours ahead of you), especially mine!!!! I don't get enough sleep as it is! One becomes jet-lagged due to the time difference. Many people try to stay awake to combat it, but I succumbed to my body's need to sleep around 1 pm and awoke around 5:19 pm to a voice whispering, 'Treasured, Talitha Koum Arise'.

Perusing my much-loved **Mark 5:19 (NIV)** I read:
"**19** Jesus did not let him, but said, 'Go home to your own people and tell them how much the Lord has done for you, and how he has had mercy on you'."

I believe through this scripture the Lord was telling me to testify during my sermon on Sunday at FireNights The Hague event and indeed everywhere I go, about what the Lord has done for me.

The Lord said to "tell your own people". I became emotional reading this as years ago in my late twenties the Lord told me I would be a Mother to many nations. Indeed, I have loved the FireNights couple (visionaries who commenced the events) like my very own children. We labored in the vineyard together and they sent me forth, commissioning me for the work that lay ahead and beyond. The Lord gave them a rare view into my future which He had shared with me years ago and only a few prophets of the Lord have captured and confirmed the vision.

They are my very own and beloved spiritual daughter, son and grandchild. They prayed for you without knowing you were a part of my future work!

From **v21** of the same chapter. Mark writes about Jesus' encounter with the dead girl and the sick woman. This passage also has such a deep connection with my grandson's healing which I wrote about in the Release the Dove Book.

I just love scripture and would like you to read along with me for context the following:

Mark 5:35-42 (NIV)
"**35** While Jesus was still speaking, some people came from the house of Jairus, the synagogue leader. 'Your daughter is dead,' they said. 'Why bother the teacher anymore?'
36 Overhearing what they said, Jesus told him, 'Don't be afraid; just believe. '
37 He did not let anyone follow him except Peter, James and John the brother of James. **38** When they came to the home of the synagogue leader, Jesus saw a commotion, with people crying and wailing loudly. **39** He went in and said to them, 'Why all this commotion and wailing? The child is not dead but asleep.' **40** But they laughed at Him.
After he put them all out, he took the child's father and mother and the disciples who were with him, and went in where the child was.
41 He took her by the hand and said to her, .
'Talitha koum!' (which means "Little girl, I say to you, get up!"). **42** Immediately the girl stood up and began to walk around (she was twelve years old). At this they were completely astonished."

I believe the Lord is saying to us "Treasured daughters of the King, arise and go forth and testify of what Almighty God has done for us." The Little girl was 12 and the Lord also had 12 disciples! We had 12 most meetings but on the last meeting all 15 Oasis Houston daughters were accounted for!

Many do not like to tell of the mighty works the Father has wrought in their lives. Of the 10 lepers who were healed (**Luke 17: 11-19 NIV**) only one returned to say thank you to The Master! Testifying shames, the enemy and glorifies God!

The Lord is saying "Treasured or Valued daughter, stand up! Arise!" When you arise, the Lord arises and the enemies of God are defeated!

Psalms 68:1 reads: 'May God arise, may his enemies be scattered; may his foes flee before him.'

Testify of his mighty works today to someone who needs to hear of the goodness of the Lord in the Land of the living! You are the hands and feet of Jesus upon this earth! Your testimony might change a life!

Pray:
Dear Heavenly Father. I know I am your treasured possession. I will arise and tell of your mighty works. When you arise o Lord your enemies scatter, may my enemies be scattered as well in Jesus Mighty Name! Amen.

Day 12: Treasured, Talitha Koum Arise! Part II

Jesus has power over death!

Revelation 1:18 (KJV) reads:
"**18** I am he that liveth, and was dead; and, behold, I am alive for evermore, Amen; and have the keys of hell and of death."
Praise the Lord! I've only preached at one funeral and I wanted to shout because of the victory Jesus holds over death! I had prepared

so much, I had to cut it short. The Pastor of the Church met me later and wanted to hear the remainder of my sermon because of the words of life which I spoke!

1 Corinthians 15:55 (KJV) reads:
"**55** O death, where is thy sting? O grave, where is thy victory?" Jesus knew that he would be resurrected from the grave and take the keys of sin and death from the devil. Death to Jesus was like sleeping.

In **John 11:11 (NKJV)** He told his disciples this:
"These things He said, and after that He said to them, "Our friend Lazarus sleeps, but I go that I may wake him up." Again, you see Jesus referring to death like sleep.

It says in **Romans 8:11 (KJV)**:
"But if the Spirit of him that raised up Jesus from the dead dwell in you, he that raised up Christ from the dead shall also quicken your mortal bodies by his Spirit that dwelleth in you."
The Holy Spirit will "quicken, awaken" our mortal bodies and bring back to life that which has been pronounced dead!

The story in **Mark 5:37-40 (NIV)** reads:
"**37** He did not let anyone follow him except Peter, James and John the brother of James. **38** When they came to the home of the synagogue leader, Jesus saw a commotion, with people crying and wailing loudly. **39** He went in and said to them. 'Why all this commotion and wailing? The child is not dead but asleep.' **40** But they laughed at him."

When my grandson was on life support the Lord would not allow the doctors to even pronounce the word "coma" to me. They said he had "decreased consciousness". His nanny said, "He's just tired, he needs to sleep." I had spoken so much about life around her she too began to speak like me! She spoke faith!To become a disciple of Christ or to follow him as a Rabbi simply means, "Come be like me". You must get to the place whereby you can see things the way Jesus sees them! I too put all naysayers and unbelievers out of the room. I only kept two people with me. I needed their faith level to be high in order to receive the miraculous from God for my grandson to live.

That same Spirit that raised Jesus from the dead lives in us! Speak life over dead situations. Speak and see death as He did! Treasured, Talitha Koum, Arise! In one of Reinhard Bonnke's services in Nigeria, a woman brought her husband's dead corpse into his service because she believed with all her heart he would return to life, and he did! **Hebrews 11:35a (NIV)** says: "Women received back their dead, raised to life again."

Pray:
Lord, you do not see death as death but only as sleeping. I am your treasured disciple and want to see things as you see them. I want to speak life over everything that is dead or sleeping around me (Speak those things out-loud whether over people or situations). With conviction and radical faith say 'Talitha Koum, Arise!'

Day 13: The Power of Community

The Bible says in **Hebrews 10:25 (NLT)**:
"And let us not neglect our meeting together, as some people do, but encourage one another, especially now that the day of his return is drawing near." I mentioned in the Release the Dove book how Community played such a pivotal role in my grandson's healing by ensuring that my family and my needs were taken care of. One of my leading ladies and right hand 'sister' Barb put the wheels in motion for me to have a place to stay in Singapore. We had the most

gracious host and hostess anyone could ever ask for Shereen & William Costley.

My prayer walking partner Carol organized daily intercessory prayers on her end and one of my Leading ladies Loma kept Oasis going. Mind you, I did not request any of this to be done, it was done out of the goodness of their hearts! In Acts 2 it talks about how the early believers dwelled together.

The Fellowship of the Believers.
Acts 2:42-47 (NIV): "**42** They devoted themselves to the apostles' teaching and to fellowship, to the breaking of bread and to prayer. **43** Everyone was filled with awe at the many wonders and signs performed by the apostles. **44** All the believers were together and had everything in common. **45** They sold property and possessions to give to anyone who had need. **46** Every day they continued to meet together in the temple courts. They broke bread in their homes and ate together with glad and sincere hearts, **47** praising God and enjoying the favor of all the people. And the Lord added to their number daily those who were being saved."

I know what you are thinking, because I've always felt the same thing coming from a Capitalist country. Just how can we live out this fellowship Principle without feeling we are losing our individuality?

I was extremely touched when I visited my hometown last month and my friend Anita Smalley insisted, I stay with them. Her husband Brent actually built the beautiful unique barn house they are living in! He also built my bed with his hands the week I was coming! They now call their spare bedroom "Rhonda's room".

Community is such an integral part of my lifestyle now; I simply don't live without it.

Pray:
Father, please help me understand more in regard to this Fellowship Principle as I wish to be more of Service to the Community in which I live as well as my Church family. In Jesus Name Amen.

Day 14 - Being tempted is not the same as Falling into sin

We're two weeks into our 40-day fast and it has come to my attention that many might be struggling with this fast! I know I certainly am!!! The enemy and your flesh know exactly how to tempt you. Don't go there! Just don't!
Jesus was tempted by Satan but didn't sin.
"For we do not have a high priest who is unable to empathize with our weaknesses, but we have one who has been tempted in every way, just as we are—yet was without sin". **Hebrews 4:15 (NIV)** .

When Jesus was fasting for 40 days and in the wilderness, the enemy went to him and tried to provoke him to temptation. Jesus did NOT sin. How did He respond to the temptation? By quoting scripture.

Matthew 4:4-6 (NLV) (Used more simple translation today)
"**4** But Jesus said, "It is written, 'Man is not to live on bread only. Man is to live by every word that God speaks.'"
5 Then the devil took Jesus up to Jerusalem, the holy city. He had Jesus stand on the highest part of the house of God.
6 The devil said to Him, "If You are the Son of God, throw Yourself down. It is written, 'He has told His angels to look after You. In their hands they will hold You up. Then Your foot will not hit against a stone.'" (Used simple translation today.) Please notice that the enemy also knew scripture and used it, but Jesus did not succumb to the temptation.

Pray:
Lord Jesus, help me against this battle of my flesh. You were also tempted, Lord Jesus yet you did not sin. I release these temptations into your capable hands. I desire to stay the course and finish strong, in Jesus Name, Amen!

Day 15 – Letting go of Fear of the Coronavirus I

Listen to what **Hebrews 4:12 (NIV)** says:
"For the word of God is alive and active. Sharper than any double-edged sword, it penetrates even to dividing soul and spirit, joints and marrow; it judges the thoughts and attitudes of the heart."
I love God's Word because it is alive, and it never returns void but accomplishes the purpose it was sent.

Here in Europe, like America I'm sure, there is a scarcity of sanitizer gel and masks, people are stripping the grocery store shelves bare. There is nothing wrong with preparation. I'm a planner myself! But when it's motivated by fear and you are a child of God, you need to re-think your position in Christ.

Please read with me these passages of scripture in Exodus, pay close attention and underline the following verses in the three points that follow.

Exodus 9:13-26 (NIV):
"The Plague of Hail
13 Then the Lord said to Moses, 'Get up early in the morning, confront Pharaoh and say to him, 'This is what the Lord, the God of the Hebrews, says: Let my people go, so that they may worship me, **14** or this time I will send the full force of my plagues against you and against your officials and your people, so you may know that there is

no one like me in all the earth. **15** For by now I could have stretched out my hand and struck you and your people with a plague that would have wiped you off the earth. **16** But I have raised you up[a] for this very purpose, that I might show you my power and that my name might be proclaimed in all the earth. **17** You still set yourself against my people and will not let them go. **18** Therefore, at this time tomorrow I will send the worst hailstorm that has ever fallen on Egypt, from the day it was founded till now. **19** Give an order now to bring your livestock and everything you have in the field to a place of shelter, because the hail will fall on every person and animal that has not been brought in and is still out in the field, and they will die.' **20** Those officials of Pharaoh who feared the word of the Lord hurried to bring their slaves and their livestock inside. **21** But those who ignored the word of the Lord left their slaves and livestock in the field.

22 Then the Lord said to Moses, 'Stretch out your hand toward the sky so that hail will fall all over Egypt—on people and animals and on everything growing in the fields of Egypt.' **23** When Moses stretched out his staff toward the sky, the Lord sent thunder and hail, and lightning flashed down to the ground. So the Lord rained hail on the land of Egypt; **24** hail fell and lightning flashed back and forth. It was the worst storm in all the land of Egypt since it had become a nation. **25** Throughout Egypt hail struck everything in the fields—both people and animals; it beat down everything growing in the fields and stripped every tree. **26** The only place it did not hail was the land of Goshen, where the Israelites were."

1- **verse 16** - God's purpose was not to destroy them rather the Lord wanted to show his power so that his name is Glorified throughout the earth. They were raised up to fulfill their God given purpose.

2- **verse 19 -** God is a merciful God. He still instructed the Egyptians to bring in their livestock to shelter in order not to be destroyed by the plague.
3- **verse 26** - The only place the hail did not strike was in the land of Goshen where the people of God resided!

Listen, Listen dear Ones. We are under a Covenant of protection. We should not fear the same way the world does rather we should plead that the plague stops so people and nations are not destroyed. We should reverence the Word of God and seek discernment in What God wants you do upon the earth.

Remember He does nothing without first revealing it to his prophets or servants. **Amos 3:7**.

The purpose of the plagues in Exodus was not to utterly destroy them but to get their attention and for the Lord's name to be glorified.

Pray:
Lord I Release fear of the unknown. You just told me you would do nothing upon the earth without first revealing it to your prophets and servants. Lord we are your handmaidens listening and ready to act according to your will. We ask for forgiveness on behalf of the nations, Lord.

Your Word declares there is nothing new under the sun therefore we pray for a cure for Covid-19 Virus Lord. We decree that Covid-19 is stopped in its tracks. In Jesus mighty Name, Amen!

Testimony | Carol Smart

Being completely honest I didn't see how I was going to pull it off. I was attending college at the time, and the "Release the Dove" study was being held at seven p.m. every Tuesday. an hour's drive away from my home. My regular bedtime is somewhere between Eight and Nine p.m. But the biggest issue for me was that I would have to drive at night, which literally frightened me to no end. When I woke up on Tuesday mornings the anxiety began. I knew in just a few hours I would be faced with the task of driving on the I 10 in Houston, Texas. I would pray and ask the Lord to take the anxiety from me and replace it with complete trust in Him knowing that He cares for me and sees me right where I am, **ref; Jeremiah 29:11.**

My understanding of trust and faith is that they are intertwined with each other, without one you can't have the other. **"Release the Dove"** *is a complete study on trust and faith. Faith that God will do what He said He would do. He promised to never leave us or forsake us.* **Deuteronomy 31:6** *says, "Be strong and of good courage, do not fear nor be afraid of them; for the LORD your God, He is the One who goes with you. He will not leave you nor forsake you." I clung onto that truth throughout the study. The driving and the late nights, knowing that God had me in this season for a reason. Little did I know, or could I have ever understood, what was coming almost immediately after* **"Release the Dove"** *study. A phrase that would never be forgotten, was literally on the tongue of every person in the entire world. COVID-19, Coronavirus a Global Pandemic had fallen upon every household's understanding. Kings and rulers, the rich and poor alike were given a mandate and were quarantined to stay in* *their homes and away from groups of people for weeks and then months. While I sit writing this devotional we, as a One Global Nation have no idea when the quarantine will be lifted, or when we will once again have the freedom to join our friends and family in person, instead of on video calls.*

*What does this have to do with **"Release the Dove Study?"** Everything! Through both seasons of **"Release The Dove"** study, I've learned that I must trust God with absolutely everything. My husband's life and my life also. My husband is in the high-risk group for COVID-19, which simply means that if he's stricken by the "Invisible Enemy," it would be fatal for him, but God! God has us in His loving hands, Psalm 91. My faith has grown tremendously throughout **"Release The Dove"** study season. The last night of the study Mrs. Rhonda called for a forty day fast, not knowing that soon we would all be facing an "invisible enemy." So, I set myself apart from the world and all of its pleasures, and dove deep into the Word of God with prayer and fasting. Through this season God has given me peace beyond all understanding, mixed with joy unspeakable. My trust has grown immensely and I rely on God's understanding and not my own.*

*I encourage you to read if you have not already read, **"Release the Dove"** book and bible study. It is the testimony of the unfailing love of a grandmother for her grandson, who was in the throes of death and her unwavering faith and trust that God would do exactly what He said He would do. I promise that you will be encouraged and come to a greater understanding of trust and faith that is spoken of in Proverbs 3:5,6.*

Much love, Carol Smart

Reflections

He says, "Be still, and know that I am God; I will be exalted among the nations, I will be exalted in the earth."

Psalms 46:10 NIV

Day 16 – Letting go of Fear to Praise the Lord II

The Lord inhabits the praises of His people! When the praises go up, the blessings come down! There is no room for fear in God's presence!

Psalms 22:3 (KJV):
"But thou art holy, O thou that inhabitest the praises of Israel."
The Lord told Pharaoh through his servant Moses, "Let my people go so they can go to the wilderness and worship me." (Paraphrased). **Exodus 8:1**.

Exodus 3:18b (NIV): "let us take a 3-day journey into the wilderness to offer sacrifices to the Lord our God."
He told Moses he would return to Mount Sinai to worship him. **Exodus 3:12**.

Have you been to the mountaintop today? Have you experienced the Shechinah Glory of Almighty? "Shechinah" is a transliteration of a Hebrew Word meaning "dwelling" or settling of the "divine" presence of God.

The Lord said if we did not praise him the rocks would cry out on our behalf! (paraphrased from **Luke 19:40**).

The Lord delivered the Israelites exactly when He planned on it! In **Genesis 15:16 (NIV):** He told Abram, "And then, In the fourth generation your descendants will come back here, for the sins of the Amorites has not yet reached its full measure."

God has a divine timetable and a purpose for all things. His timing is impeccable. He is never late, always on time. He is a Covenant

Keeping God! You can be certain that all His promises are Yes and Amen! Let go of fear today! God's got you!

The Lord raised up Moses not when he was in the Palace being reared by Pharaoh's daughter but when he was 80 years old on the backside of the desert tending sheep. God desires our undivided attention.

The First thing He wanted the Israelites to do after 400+ years of slavery was to come aside and spend time in his presence. To worship and to sacrifice to Him.

What have we allowed to carry us into bondage? Fear, doubt, worry and unbelief? God is inviting us to a Mountaintop experience.

During these 40 days of fasting, He wants to carry us to the Secret Place to praise him and experience a refreshing in His presence. There is no room for fear on the mountain of God. The only fear you will have is to reverence Almighty.
He revealed Himself to Moses in a Burning Bush. He told Moses He was: "I Am who I Am."

He is saying to you today:
1- I am joy
2- I Am strength
3- I Am healing
4- I am Deliverance
5- I Am Comfort
6- I Am a Way Maker
7- I am a burden lifter
8- I Am solution

Come on Sisters, what you need, God's got it! He's gently calling you into the Secret Place, into freedom, out of bondage.

He wants to hide you in the cleft of a rock as He passes by, you can see his back side and know He's got your back in every situation.

Exodus 34:6-8 (KJV):
"**6** And the Lord passed by before him, and proclaimed, The Lord, The Lord God, merciful and gracious, long suffering, and abundant in goodness and truth, **7** Keeping mercy for thousands, forgiving iniquity and transgression and sin, and that will by no means clear the guilty; visiting the iniquity of the fathers upon the children, and upon the children's children, unto the third and to the fourth generation. **8** And Moses made haste, and bowed his head toward the earth, and worshipped."

Pray:
Dear Lord Jesus, I too would like to offer up a sacrifice unto you. Whether it's what I'm giving up on this fast i.e. a habit, finances, food, FB, TV, fear of the unknown; whatever it is I want to sacrifice unto thee. The benefits of praising you and basking in your Shechinah glory far outweighs my sacrifice! Thank you, Abba, for passing by today!! I would like to break the generational curse of ————(list) off of my family and my posterity. I accept your Covenant of Peace, In Jesus Mighty Name, Amen.

Day 17 – Letting go of Fear, receive God's Insurance – His Protection Plan Part III

Psalm 91 has long been a beloved Psalm of my family and I ever since the Lord used it to deliver us from a war-torn Congo.

Huddled together in my Congo living room was a group of diverse people from different ethnicities. There was a Pastor with his wife and four children residing in our upper room, my brother-in-law and his pregnant wife who had fled the war on the evening of their wedding were living in our main home along with my husband's Professor from University and various others. The year was 1997.

On that evening, we called a prayer meeting and my sister-in-law read from Psalm 91. Afterwards, in one voice, we proclaimed safety and security for all those staying under our roof. Curiously enough, her husband had not joined in the prayers. Most of our guests had fled the Capital City of Brazzaville and had stayed in the forest until they were able to make safe passage to the Oil Capital of Pointe Noire where we lived.

We were well into our second week since the war had commenced yet it seemed to me like an eternity. The constant gunfire and bombs exploding loudly were enough to rattle one's peace. The uncertainty of what tomorrow may bring was also a concern, as I personally had informed all the Americans to leave the country (acting in the role of USA Honorary Consulate). I had chosen to stay behind with my husband and family knowing our leaving would not only mean destruction for our home but certain death for some of our guests who were from the tribe being hunted down. They had come under our roof seeking protection and security, with the help of the Lord, my husband and I were determined to provide them with just that. Thus, on that fateful evening, we all slept knowing that come what may, we were under the protection of the Father.

When the next day dawned, our home was mistakenly attacked by the French Army. They fired upon our home with the intention of killing every soul under our roof! I cried out to the Lord and he sent a rescue angel on our behalf! Even my brother-in-law who had refused to join us in prayer and was locked outside accidentally, God still protected! Not one person under our roof was hurt!

Now this is the best insurance policy I have seen to date!

Let's speak out loud Psalm 91 as a prayer:

*1 Whoever dwells in the shelter of the Most High
will rest in the shadow of the Almighty.
2 I will say of the Lord, "He is my refuge and my fortress,
my God, in whom I trust."
3 Surely he will save you
from the fowler's snare
and from the deadly pestilence.
4 He will cover you with his feathers,
and under his wings you will find refuge;
his faithfulness will be your shield and rampart.
5 You will not fear the terror of night,
nor the arrow that flies by day,
6 nor the pestilence that stalks in the darkness,
nor the plague that destroys at midday.
7 A thousand may fall at your side,
ten thousand at your right hand,
but it will not come near you.
8 You will only observe with your eyes
and see the punishment of the wicked.
9 If you say, "The Lord is my refuge,"
and you make the Most High your dwelling,
10 no harm will overtake you,
no disaster will come near your tent.
11 For he will command his angels concerning you
to guard you in all your ways;
12 they will lift you up in their hands,
so that you will not strike your foot against a stone.
13 You will tread on the lion and the cobra;
you will trample the great lion and the serpent.
14 "Because he[b] loves me," says the Lord, "I will rescue him;
I will protect him, for he acknowledges my name.
15 He will call on me, and I will answer him;*

*I will be with him in trouble,
I will deliver him and honor him.*
16 *With long life I will satisfy him
and show him my salvation."*

In Jesus Mighty Name, we have prayed. Amen.

Day 18 – God Reveals His Plans to His Servants

"Then the LORD said, 'Shall I hide from Abraham what I am about to do?'" **Genesis 18:17 (NIV).**

A careful reading of this exchange between Abraham and the 'The Lord' in Genesis 18 reveals how the Lord lovingly shared with his confidant Abraham his plans to destroy Sodom and Gomorrah because of their grievous sins. It also shows Abraham's intercession on behalf of this city because his nephew Lot and his family lived there. Before God does a "Thing" upon the earth, He reveals it to a man or a woman, His servants. Sometimes it is because He looks for us to intercede on behalf of a nation.

Ezekiel 22:30 (NIV) says:
"I looked for someone among them who would build up the wall and stand before me in the gap on behalf of the land so I would not have to destroy it, but I found no one."

Isaiah 59:16 (NIV): "He saw that there was no one, he was appalled that there was no one to intervene; so, his own arm achieved salvation for him, and his own righteousness sustained him."

I do not know about you but when reading those passages, my heart begins to burst with compassion and pump with urgency and I instantly want to cry out for the oppressed. This is a sign of intercession which moves you to pray not only for your family but for someone else and in this instance —nations suffering from this pandemic!

All in one voice sisters, God has given us the heart of an intercessor to plead the cause of nations upon the Earth in which we live. Let us take back our rightful position as custodians upon this earth and breathe life where Covid-19 is breathing death by weakening the respiratory system of its victims.

Let's cry out to the Lord right now!

Pray:
Death to Covid-19 in the mighty Name of Jesus! Whether it comes by way of Divine Intervention or by God giving knowledge to the Scientists or doctors, we are asking for a halt, a stop in the Mighty Name of Jesus. When the Israelites crossed the Red Sea, it appeared an impossibility, yet you dried up the Red Sea and the People of God crossed over on dry ground. This pandemic is too grand for man alone, just like the Red sea was an impossibility, yet Lord, you made a way. We call upon your divine intervention, Heavenly Father, or else we would all be destroyed.

We know your plan is not for complete destruction as the gospel must be preached! We command this plague to be arrested right now in Jesus Mighty Name. And when it happens, we will give you glory and honor. Experts are saying it will take 6 months before we can even begin to see change yet God, YOU are the REAL expert, therefore, we cry out for Your Divine Wisdom and Grace, In JESUS MIGHTY NAME, AMEN!

Day 19 – Releasing the Kingdom of God upon the Earth

Greetings Beloved, we are almost halfway through our 40 day fast/Devotional! What a time to be alive to witness Bible prophecy unfold before our very eyes. Yet, I hear the Lord saying to us "Do not fear, little flock, for it is your Father's good pleasure to give you the kingdom." **Luke 12:32 (NKJV)**

In the verses prior, Jesus was teaching his disciples not to worry, our heavenly Father would provide clothing, food, virtually all that we require to live. Then in **verse 31 (NIV)**, Jesus says," But seek his kingdom, and these things will be given to you as well."

According to the Matthew J. Henry Commentary on the Whole Bible, this passage centers on worldly concerns like worry or anxiety, temptations most of us face. Jesus warned His disciples about worldly concerns often, and we counter them by seeking God and His righteousness.

Jesus is saying that when we seek the Kingdom of God, and His will, earthly things pale in view of it. When we keep an eternal perspective, we can live each day as a Bonafide Ambassador representing the Kingdom of God! We can be light and salt to the world, dispelling fear and flavorless news. We can bring life into dead situations. This is the reality of the Kingdom of God!

Romans 14:17a (NIV) reads, "For the kingdom of God is not a matter of eating and drinking, but of righteousness, peace and joy in the Holy Spirit."

The Lord's prayer encourages us to pray, 'Your Kingdom come, your will be done, on earth as it is in heaven."

In the Release the Dove Study, I encouraged the participants to Release the Holy Spirit over a situation and watch it change. That we should seek God's will on every occasion and execute to the best of our God given ability.

For the first time in my life that I can remember, Churches are closed all over the world. I have believed in my heart that Christians would return to the fundamental Home Churches that commenced the Churches as we know them today.

In the book of Acts, Christians gathered in a home setting and worshipped God. Tomorrow, we will be meeting with a small group of my beloved sisters in Holland to share a meal and fellowship together. To encourage one another in the Word and to spur one another's faith in our God given purpose. This is NOT time to faint Dear One, for these are just the beginning of birth pains.

2 Corinthians 4:1 (NIV) reads:
1 "Therefore, since through God's mercy we have this ministry, we do not lose heart."
Paul continues in **verses 16-18:**
16 "Therefore we do not lose heart. Though outwardly we are wasting away, yet inwardly we are being renewed day by day. **17** For our light and momentary troubles are achieving for us an eternal glory that far outweighs them all. **18** So we fix our eyes not on what is seen, but on what is unseen, since what is seen is temporary, but what is unseen is eternal."

Tomorrow, we will look further into **Luke 12**. But today, in my role as medical personnel, I would like to provide you with some practical advice. We should in no way ignore the guidelines given by the CDC, but we should adhere to them considering the faith we have in Jesus Christ. I have attached two links for your perusal which I find may be helpful to you and your family. If you are blessed, pass them on (the links were delivered via FB. I leave this paragraph purposefully knowing that we can sometimes be zealous and ignore the wisdom of the professionals. The Lord gives us discernment in every situation).

Pray:
Heavenly Father, we receive your Words of Life with Gratitude. May your will be done on earth as it is in heaven. Teach me to trust you more. Forgive me for worrying excessively. I release the Kingdom of God upon this earth, in my home, neighborhood, Church, Children's school, in Jesus Name Amen.

Note from the author:
The photograph directly below are some of the ladies in our Houston Oasis Study. Susanne Salg far left bottom is our Oasis founder. The precious photo on the right is of me and two "daughters" during a trip to Ghana, Africa in October 2018.

Reflections

Day 20 - 2001 – The Year of my Consecration

I stood on the Podium at Double Portion Church in Northport, Alabama. It was here I had been baptized, delivered, filled with the Holy Spirit. My husband and I had gotten married in my beloved Church years ago and here I stood for my ordination ceremony.

Prior to going to Congo, I had been commissioned and sent forth to preach the gospel but now the Pastors wanted to make things more official. The Assistant Pastor's hands shook, as she helped perform the ceremony and I could see she was not at ease. I wondered about her apprehension but decided to wait to question her later.

We had already spent much time together on the Mission Field in Africa when she had stayed in my home. Her doors were always open for my family and I to stay when I returned to the USA as well. We loved one another dearly. Therefore, I could not fathom why she did not appear happy for me nor did I understand her hesitation.

The next day, we met for lunch and there she shared with me the dream she had had. She dreamt there had been a Terrorist attack therefore she felt strongly that I should not travel. In fact, she felt imminent danger. I too had had a dream about a plane crash which I also shared with her. In the back of my mind, I thought all of this had to do with her dislike of flying that she was now projecting on to me. Yet, I also knew the power of prophecy, Word of Knowledge and anointing that my Pastor carried so gracefully. It was her prophecies that I was living out that very moment! Therefore, I took heed to her advice but did not cancel my flight.

My flight was on September 11, 2001, my twins needed to get back to school in Gamba, Gabon. Besides, I had purchased tickets that were at a special rate whereby change was not allowed. I let her know about my dream but felt God would protect us come what may.

We had survived the war in 97 and I knew we could endure anything! The morning of September 11, 2001 dawned as any ordinary travel day for me. I had 6 large suitcases and one carry-on luggage. I busied myself packing, weighing the suitcases and repacking which was my custom.

I had settled the children in the back bedroom watching cartoons whilst I completed my packing and travel preparations. We were staying in my brother's home which was very close to the airport. He had planned to collect me a couple of hours before my flight and drop me at the small airport a few miles away. I chose not to turn the television on in the living room nor did I play the radio. I had made the decision to travel despite my Pastor's warning and my own dream. I simply wanted to get home but could not shake my uneasiness nor her words. She had never been wrong before.

As the day wore on, I began to get phone messages as well as missed calls which I ignored. I could hear the constant beeps indicating messages were coming in on my phone. Thinking back, I suppose I simply did not want to hear any bad news. My mind had been made up about my travel plans. Finally, right before my brother was to come, I answered my sister's call who wanted to know where in the world I had been and why I hadn't responded to her calls. She inquired whether I was watching the news. Something in her tone of voice persuaded me to turn on the television then the horrific truth of the day unfolded.

God had spoken to his servant, Sis Sarah and he had spoken to me. The Lord had also preserved us in the time of trouble. I knew that our future was secure in His Hands.

Psalm 27:5 (NIV):
"For in the day of trouble he will keep me safe in his dwelling; he will hide me in the shelter of his sacred tent and set me high upon a rock."

Pray:
Lord, you know my going in and my coming out. You know my end from my beginning. You have hemmed me in protecting me from hurt, harm and danger. You Lord are the King of Israel and you neither sleep nor slumber, but you watch over me. For in the day of trouble You will keep me safe in your dwelling; You will hide me in the shelter of your sacred tent and set me high upon a rock. Thank you, O Lord, for covering my family and I, my Church, my neighborhood, our nation and all the nations of the world. Thank you, Lord, for guiding the Head of States to making the right decisions for their nations at a time such as this. In Jesus Mighty Name, Amen.

Day 21 – A Sudden Halt!

As suddenly as destruction started it will cease!

In the time of Elisha, there was a terrible famine in Samaria. Ben-Hadad king of Aram had laid siege to Samaria and there was terrible famine in the Land. The siege lasted so long that a donkey's head sold for eighty shekels of silver, and a quarter of a cab of seed pods for five shekels. It was so bad the king was called to settle a dispute between two women who planned to kill and eat their sons.

The wicked king was angry with Elisha although he knew the predicament of the land was due to their sin, but he also realized Elisha had power with God! Elisha showed up in the nick of time with this incredible message of Grace from the Lord. We pick up this story in **2 Kings 7: 1-2 (NIV):**

"**1** Elisha replied, 'Hear the word of the Lord. This is what the Lord says: "About this time tomorrow, a seah[a] of the finest flour will sell for a shekel and two seah's of barley for a shekel at the gate of Samaria." **2** The officer on whose arm the king was leaning said to the man of God, 'Look, even if the Lord should open the floodgates of the heavens, could this happen?' 'You will see it with your own eyes,' answered Elisha, 'but you will not eat any of it!'"

Elisha came to announce the end of the famine, a 24-hour turn around! The king believed but his officer did not! The word was fulfilled the very next day just as Elisha prophesied, however the officer was trampled by the multitude rushing into the city to purchase food. He died because of unbelief. This is NOT our portion in Jesus name!

For a few days now, I have heard the word "Sudden" in my spirit. As suddenly as CoronaVirus started and swept over the earth it will also cease. The Bible declares in **Job 22:28-29 (KJV):**
"**28**Thou shalt also decree a thing, and it shall be established unto thee: and the light shall shine upon thy ways."

In **verse 28** it says we should decree or declare a thing and it will be established. Webster's definition of 'to establish' means to institute (something, such as a law) permanently by enactment or agreement.

The very next verse tells us to speak differently than the world:
29 When men are cast down, then thou shalt say, "There is lifting up; and he shall save the humble person."

This is not merely positive speaking; this is declaring the Word as God does! How many will believe with me for a sudden halt of Corona?

2 Chronicles 29:36 (KJV): "And Hezekiah rejoiced, and all the people, that God had prepared the people: for the thing was done suddenly."

Pray:
Abba Father, your will be done on earth as it is in heaven. In heaven there is no sickness, there is no CoronaVirus, there is no death. I decree and declare, CoronaVirus must Halt, Stop, Cease Suddenly, In Jesus Mighty Name! Amen!

If you believe it dear One, then it is done!

Day 22 – Watch and Pray

On Day 18, we read from **Luke 12**, I promised to pick up from where we left off after my slight little detour. This morning let's look at **verses 35-40 (NIV)** which speak on Watchfulness.

Watchfulness – simply means to be expectant, looking, standing in faith, both watching and observing the times as well as praying:
35 "Be dressed ready for service and keep your lamps burning, **36** like servants waiting for their master to return from a wedding banquet, so that when he comes and knocks, they can immediately open the door for him. **37** It will be good for those servants whose master finds them watching when he comes. Truly I tell you, he will dress himself to serve, will have them recline at the table and will come and wait on them. **38** It will be good for those servants whose master finds them ready, even if he comes in the middle of the night or toward daybreak. **39** But understand this: If the owner of the house had known at what hour the thief was coming, he would not

have let his house be broken into. **40** You also must be ready, because the Son of Man will come at an hour when you do not expect him."

This is a parable that Jesus told to his disciples about His Second Coming. So grateful to Doctor Luke (who also wrote The Book of Acts and the only Gentile to write any part of the New Testament) for recording this to instruct us during our current lifestyle and understanding.

These verses warn us to keep our lamps burning. **Psalms 119:105 (NLT)** reads, 'Your word is a lamp to guide my feet and a light for my path.' Then **Psalm 37:23 (NLT)** reads: "The LORD directs the steps of the godly. He delights in every detail of their lives."

I searched windowinthebible.com to see whether there was anything spiritual to glean from lamps used in Jesus Day.

This is what I found out:
Lamps used by the Jews at the time of Jesus were extremely plain. These Herodian lamps lacked any decoration as the pious Jews banned the use of most images on their objects.

They did however still retain the functional innovations of the Greeks. I discovered they were simply functional whereby olive oil, fish or lard was used to ignite the lamps to help light up a room, a path or a dark place. Although these ancient lamps did not cast much light on a path, God's Word does. His Word instructs us on how to live. The oil is symbolic of the Holy Spirit which guides us into all truth **(John 16:13).**

We can easily discern why Jesus often used lamps in his parables or teachings. For example, in **Matthew 25:1-13**, he tells the parable about ten virgins. There were five wise virgins who kept oil in their lamps and kept their lamps burning whilst watching, praying and waiting for the Bridegroom - symbolic of Jesus' Second Coming. The five foolish virgins did not. But at the time of Jesus' Second Coming they all slept but woke up at his return!

Those who Jesus KNEW and whose lamps were burning, he took with him into the wedding feast (heaven) but the five foolish virgins who professed to know Christ were not known by Him. It is one thing to profess faith in Christ, but it is altogether another matter to be bearing the fruit of the Spirit, revealing that you are truly abiding in the vine **(John 15:7).**

Matthew 7:21-23 warns "Not everyone who says to me, 'Lord, Lord,' will enter the kingdom of heaven, but the one who does the will of my Father who is in heaven. On that day many will say to me, 'Lord, Lord, did we not prophesy in your name, and cast out demons in your name, and do many mighty works in your name?' And then will I declare to them, 'I never knew you; depart from me, you workers of lawlessness.'"

The use of the double "Lord, Lord" is a sign of intimacy in Jewish literature. One of my dear mentees who had also been one of my Pastors said intimacy means "in-to-me". When you are "in-to-Christ" you are busy spending time with him, learning about him, talking to him and doing His will.

I pray these parables serve as "Wake Up" calls for all of us.

Let us Pray:
Dear Heavenly Father may my lamp always be lit with the oil of gladness and joy in the Holy Spirit. I willingly hand over the reins of my life – all of it - for you to guide me down the path of righteousness. I want to be like the Wise Virgin, the Wise Believer who kept my lamp burning in anticipation of your return. Even if I

sleep, I know when you return, I will hear your voice and you will raise me up on the last day! Thank you, Lord Jesus. In your name. Amen.

Revelation 22:17 (NKJV): "The Spirit and the bride say, "Come!" And let the one who hears him say, "Come!" Let the one who thirsts come. Whoever desires, let him take the water of life freely."

Day 23– A National Day of Prayer

The Netherlands proclaimed a National Day of Prayer in March 2020. Hallelujah somebody! In one voice, we gathered as a nation to pray to Almighty on behalf of this nation and for its people and for the cessation of the Covid-19.

The Bible declares in **Jeremiah 29:7 (NIV):** "Also, seek the peace and prosperity of the city to which I have carried you into exile. Pray to the LORD for it, because if it prospers, you too will prosper."

Therefore, whatever nation, state, city, town or village you are in right now, pray for it. You ought to pray for people in leadership as **2 Timothy 2:2 (NLT)** recommends: "Pray this way for kings and all who are in authority so that we can live peaceful and quiet lives marked by godliness and dignity."

You see, praying for them is also good for our well-being and welfare! We can observe in **Jonah 3 (KJV)** what happens to a nation in conflict. Jonah was sent to Nineveh to announce the destruction of their city. He reluctantly went halfheartedly proclaiming the Word of the Lord. This is what happened! **Jonah 3:4-10 (KJV):** "**4** And Jonah began to enter into the city a day's journey, and he cried, and said, 'yet forty days, and Nineveh shall be overthrown.'
5 So the people of Nineveh believed God, and proclaimed a fast, and

put on sackcloth, from the greatest of them even to the least of them.
6 For word came unto the king of Nineveh, and he arose from his throne, and he laid his robe from him, and covered him with sackcloth, and sat in ashes.
7 And he caused it to be proclaimed and published through Nineveh by the decree of the king and his nobles, saying, 'Let neither man nor beast, herd nor flock, taste any thing: let them not feed, nor drink water:
8 But let man and beast be covered with sackcloth, and cry mightily unto God: yea, let them turn everyone from his evil way, and from the violence that is in their hands.
9 Who can tell if God will turn and repent, and turn away from his fierce anger, that we perish not?'
10 And God saw their works, that they turned from their evil way; and God repented of the evil, that he had said that he would do unto them; and he did it not."

I simply love this story in the Bible. Not only does it depict the power of prayer but the goodness of Almighty God! Nineveh was the ancient capital of the Assyrian empire.
The whole entire book of Nahum outlines God's judgment against the Assyrians but the book of Jonah deals with the theme of God showing mercy on Assyrians regardless of their cruelty.
When hearing the proclamation and decree of Jonah, the King Himself, laid in sackcloth and fasted! Even the animals and children fasted!

Jonah's message was simple, "Yet forty days and Nineveh shall be overthrown". Destruction was certain for this great city as God had sent a warning message through his servant Jonah. Jonah knew the Lord. He did not want to go and preach in Nineveh because he knew God as being loving, kind and full of grace and mercy. He knew if the people fasted and prayed, God would hear!

Sisters, we are on this 40-day journey at a most opportune time to bring Christ's will to the earth. Though Jonah preached destruction in 40 days, let us discern from the Word of God in **Jeremiah 1:10 (NLT):** "Today I appoint you to stand up against nations and kingdoms. Some you must uproot and tear down, destroy and overthrow. Others you must build up and plant."

Join me during this National Day of Prayer in the city wherever you are to appeal to Almighty God on behalf of your city. Pray for Leadership, their wellbeing and their governance. Pray for salvation of your city and against whatever crime or issue may be plaguing your city at this time. We have a loving and Kind God who not only hears but acts!

Photo below: My Dutch friend Cynthia and I took a prayer walk on this National Day of Prayer. When we reached the highest point above the sea while standing on a cliff of a rock, I made some decrees over the city and prayed according to **Jeremiah 29:7** *"Also, seek the peace and prosperity of the city to which I have carried you into exile. Pray to the Lord for it, because if it prospers, you too will prosper."*

Day 24 – The Latter-Day Harvest is Ripe!

I love where our home is situated in The Netherlands, close to the North Sea. Over the years, my husband and I have enjoyed many weekends, walking on the beach exploring the nearby shops, stalls and restaurants. This trip, I have had the privilege of taking long walks with various friends. I cherish our one-on-one conversations.

On one such occasion, a friend was telling me about a dream she had had this week. She was standing all alone in a field and the harvest was ripe! She looked around at the harvest and said, "Lord, I'm not an evangelist, I'm not accustomed to preaching the gospel. I'm not even so good at telling people about you," she exclaimed. "Why have you placed me in this field?"

How we interpret and discern the times is key in understanding what God is doing. In **Luke 12:54-56 (NIV)**, Jesus was addressing the audience:

Interpreting the Times
54 "He said to the crowd: 'When you see a cloud rising in the west, immediately you say, "It's going to rain," and it does. **55** And when the south wind blows, you say, "It's going to be hot," and it is. **56** Hypocrites! You know how to interpret the appearance of the earth and the sky. How is it that you don't know how to interpret this present time?"

You see my friend Mary thought she needed a gift or a special title to speak to people about Jesus. But she IS a firebrand! Just being in her presence, you can tell Jesus radiates from her countenance! She told the Lord that she was willing to be used in his "Latter Day Harvest".

God's not looking for **JUST** Evangelists, Pastors or Prophets to preach the gospel. He wants each one of us to tell somebody about His son, Jesus Christ!

How do you interpret this present time? Many observe the times we are in and shrink back in panic and fear. People need to hear the good news! Oftentimes where there is opposition, opportunity is present! The Harvest is ripe!

One of my Bible Study ladies had a dream a few weeks back of a multitude of fish, I told her they were souls of the Latter-Day Harvest! How do you interpret these present times? The Lord of The Harvest is requesting your service. In **Luke 10:2 (NIV)** he was talking to his disciples. He told them, "The harvest is plentiful, but the workers are few. Ask the Lord of the harvest, therefore, to send out workers into his harvest field."

My husband often tells the story of how the Chinese came invading the territory of Congo during the Civil war in 1997. While Congolese were frantic or cowering in their homes, the Chinese came in setting up restaurants, stalls in the marketplace making a fortune!

Let us take the opportunity during this great opposition taking place in this world to tell somebody about Jesus. By the same token, the economy is also dwindling, ask the Lord for business ideas during this time that might bless you and somebody else!
Let's Pray:
Heavenly Father, help me to discern this present time that we are living in. You've said The Harvest is Plentiful, but the workers are few. Teach me to be like Isaiah in this generation! He said, "Send me, Lord, I'll go" Abba Father show me my harvest spiritually and financially in Jesus Mighty Name, Amen.

Day 25 - Sheep without a Shepherd

Some of you commented on the photo I posted of the plump sheep near my dwelling here in The Netherlands. Those docile sheep were peacefully grazing on the countryside oblivious to our passing.
But sheep are gregarious in nature, notorious for following the leader. They find their strength in banding together. They can graze for hours, look up and find themselves completely lost from the shepherd and the rest of the herd. Or in the case of no Shepherd, the entire flock can follow a sheep that is leading them into danger even over a cliff or into a treacherous ravine!

In **Matthew 9:35-36 (NIV) :**
"**35** Jesus went through all the towns and villages, teaching in their synagogues, proclaiming the good news of the kingdom and healing every disease and sickness. **36** When he saw the crowds, he had compassion on them, because they were harassed and helpless, like sheep without a shepherd.

In **John 10:11 (NIV)** He says: **11** "I am the good shepherd. The good shepherd lays down his life for the sheep."
The most famous shepherd we know of in the Bible was David. We saw how he literally killed the lion and the bear to protect his sheep. **(ref: 1 Samuel 17:34-36)**.

Ancient shepherds mentioned in the Bible would put their sheep in a "pen" at night and literally lay down at the "door" preventing ravenous predators from getting to their sheep. It was indeed a dangerous but heroic job being a shepherd, even if only the sheep knew and were grateful! It is interesting that my friend and fellow intercessor Kyndra had a dream about our Pastors (our Church Shepherds) sitting down in discussion this week. I believe that they were concerned about their "flock" (congregation) and were discussing possible options for leading the congregation during these perilous times.

In **John 10:14-16 (NIV)** Jesus says:
"**14** I am the good shepherd; I know my sheep and my sheep know me— **15** just as the Father knows me and I know the Father—and I lay down my life for the sheep. **16** I have other sheep that are not of this sheep pen. I must bring them also. They too will listen to my voice, and there shall be one flock and one shepherd."

It is a well-known fact that actual sheep know the voice of their shepherd and will not follow another. They will even get frightened if a stranger tries to lead them!

In the ancient Middle East, sheep would be herded into a makeshift "pen" at night, one shepherd would be designated to watch over the sheep whilst the other shepherds would go into town and get a good night's sleep. In the morning when the shepherds would return for their sheep, they would simply call out in the "pen" where there might have been hundreds of sheep and their sheep would come to them and follow! Out of hundreds of sheep, the shepherd knew his flock.

What an incredible analogy the Lord has given us in which we can be certain He will not leave us NOR forsake us. Not only that, Jesus cares about those sheep which are not yet in the pen. He wants them also to follow him. Won't you help me pray for the lost today?

Pray:
Father, today we see just how compassionate you are about the lost. You want none to perish but all to be saved. We pray for the lost sheep today O Lord. That they too shall follow you and be saved. We also pray for our Shepherds (Pastors) around the world. You are the

Good Shepherd; Abba please give your Shepherds supernatural ability to guide and navigate these difficult times in which we are in.

Lord in many scriptures we read of you going around the villages healing all sickness and disease. We beseech you Jehovah-Rophe to spread forth your healing wings over every nation afflicted by the CoronaVirus and heal them. We also pray for those who have lost loved ones or are suffering from another malady (you can call out their names) In the Name of your son Jesus Christ, Amen and Amen.

Reflections

_____

_____

_____

_____

_____

_____

_____

Testimony | Roxanne Cook

Dear Rhonda,

So, last night after Jim went to bed at 8.30 pm, I decided it was time to write the letter to my mom. I started with the Lord's prayer (from the Hope City Prayer Booklet) to prepare my heart. I asked the Holy Spirit to show me what I'm supposed to learn from this and to fill the void left. I typed it all out and added a lot of feelings I have been holding on to (fear, anger, resentment, bitterness, etc.).

- *Touched briefly on my feelings towards my mother.*
- *My son's health, I haven't told anyone, but he is having a colonoscopy done due to bleeding, waiting on the scheduling. I've let fear creep in over this.*
- *My husband's job, I hate the way he allows the words they speak over him, trample his dreams. He won't speak up and just shuts down.*
- *Continual obedience and submissiveness to Jim in our marriage*
- *Financial concerns*
- *Direction over my career*

I asked for forgiveness over all these issues, for allowing the enemy to play with my mind and asked for the Holy Spirit to speak to me. I also spent time learning the names of God and speaking them over each issue and myself.

God is my Righteousness. He makes me clean.	*Jehovah Tsidkenu*
God is my Sanctifier. He has called me and set me apart.	*Jehovah McKaddesh*
God is my Healer. He heals all my diseases.	*Jehovah Rapha*
God is my Banner of Victory. He defeated my enemies.	*Jehovah Nissi*
God is my Shepherd. He speaks to me and leads me.	*Jehovah Roah*
God is my Peace. He is my peace in EVERY storm.	*Jehovah Shalom*
God In my Provider. He supplies all of my needs.	*Jehovah Jireh*
God is my Companion. He is my friend.	*Jehovah Shammah*

*I got to page 13 - ``***Express Faith in God's Ability***"* - "*For yours is the Kingdom and the power and the glory forever." That is when the Holy Spirit spoke to me!*

I heard, **"You realize you're still going to Heaven no matter what lies you have believed from the enemy! Your life on earth will just be more difficult until you wholly believe all God's Word says! Give yourself grace, see yourself the way God sees you. He sent His son to die on the cross for you, respect (honor) that?" WOW!**

I looked at the clock on the computer to note the time. was **12:32** on **02/20/2020**!!!

I Googled the bible verse for 12:32 and it is **Luke 12:32 - Fear not, little flock; for it is your Father's good pleasure to give you the Kingdom!** Tears!!!
Then I looked at the date - 02/20/2020 - 2+2+2+2=8.

I researched the biblical meaning of 8. More confirmation from the Holy Spirit and tears:

- New Beginnings - letting go and forgiving my mother, forgiveness for my sins.
- Born Again Event into Eternal Life - Yes.
- Resurrection - my baptism.
- Regeneration - Garrett's issue, confirmation he is going to be alright! Plus my health problems.
- Balance - Spiritual vs Material - Rox.
- Material Abundance - Jim's job.
- Career Success - both Jim and I.
- Infinity Symbol (if 8 is laid on its side) - God is infinity.
- Eternity - God's promise to his believers.
- Circumcision of the heart through Christ and the receiving of the Holy Spirit - Yes.
- New Creation with Godly Character – Yes.
- Jesus proclaims if anyone is thirsty (spiritually) - they shall come to him to drink, John 7:37-39 - Yes.
- The day is divided into 8 equal parts - Night 4 / Day 4 - First, Second, Third and Fourth Watch - The Holy Spirit spoke to me during the night - Third Watch - I know full well this has a meaning!
- Jesus showed himself alive eight times after his resurrection from the dead.

- 8 people saved in the ark for new creation after the flood - God's peace covenant with us.
- 8 is the number for Jesus.
- Divine Wisdom – that's who Jesus is.
- Peace - Jesus' promise to us.
- Harmony - Yes.
- Infinite Energy & Love - My marriage.
- Compassion - Attribute of Jesus, Widow's Group, my personality.
- Self- Confidence - the Holy Spirit has renewed that in me
- Self-Discipline - what I prayed for during my 40 day fast (overspending), confirmation.
- Decisiveness - gift from the Holy Spirit.
- Gratefulness - Keep Positive Attitude - Yes
- Jesus resurrected on the 17 th day of Nissan - 1+7=8.
- The 8th day from when Jesus was selected to be sacrificed.
- Completeness - how I feel.
- God rested on the 7th day so the 8th day was new beginnings - that's what we are after Baptism.
- Elijah had 8 miracles – researching.
- Abraham had 8 agreements with God - researching.
- 8 songs mentioned in the Old Testament - researching.
- Elisha had 8 miracles - researching.
- Having left the carnal world for the spiritual world - our decision to be saved
- I learned through the Marriage Retreat this past weekend that there is no mention of bridges in the bible. Everyone went THROUGH whatever God placed before them and HE was always with them! But 8 means bridge - allowing the unsaved under the law of the Old Testament to be saved through the grace of the New Testament and Jesus' crucifixion. - Thank you, Jesus.

- Jesus was represented as the ultimate man. Jesus represents man as he needs to be in order to enter the Kingdom of God. - Yes.

I was up till 1:30! God and the Holy Spirit prepared my heart for walking through forgiveness of my mother. I slept so good last night, I didn't take my usual Tylenol or Zyrtec-D but slept soundly till 10:30 this morning! Now on to that letter to my mom!
Thanks for your prayers and for holding me accountable!

**Blessings,
Roxanne Cook**

Hope City Connect Groups - **Freedom** - Equipping you to live the victorious and abundant life Christ came to give you.

https://hopecity.churchcenter.com/groups/connect-groups/freedom-women-kty-katy-smith

Roxanne, her husband Jim and son Garrett

This is what the LORD says: "Stand at the crossroads and look; ask for the ancient paths, ask where the good way is, and walk in it, and you will find rest for your souls. But you said, 'We will not walk in it.'"

Jeremiah 6:16 NIV

Day 26 – Shun Anxiousness, put on Gratefulness, be Thankful, wear Peace

Philippians 4:6-7 (NLT): "**6** Don't worry about anything; instead, pray about everything. Tell God what you need and thank him for all he has done. **7** Then you will experience God's peace, which exceeds anything we can understand. His peace will guard your hearts and minds as you live in Christ Jesus."

I chose to use **Philippians 4:6-7 (NLT)** because it is very clear that nothing should make us anxious or worried. The very first time I attended a Bible Study in Nigeria the topic was "Walk out of Worry" by Janice Wise. Now this was during a time when I took "self-righteousness" to another level altogether!
Nevertheless, I purposed to do exactly what this verse indicated, not to worry.

This study turned my focus to trusting in God alone! You must know that whatever you are studying will be put to the test. Mine came in the midst of the study. My son was invited to participate in a triathlon organized by the school. I had vehemently refused knowing what a reckless and competitive cyclist he could be at his tender age of eight.

Besides, the event was on the Sabbath which I practiced religiously. Therefore, it was with pure dismay arriving home on the Saturday before the race that I saw a banner above our home literally begging us to allow my son to participate in the race. The message was from the Company Director's son. With a heavy heart, I prepared his bike gear for the race. His twin sister would accompany him as well as my husband. I chose to go to Church.

The next day dawned, instructions were repeated to our son how to conduct himself for the triathlon in order to remain safe. I prayed for him, repeated the instructions to my husband and went to Church. I checked my phone after service and found a message from my husband that said, "At the Hospital", nothing else. My heart did not skip a beat, I determined not to become anxious, I had given this triathlon over to the Lord.

We had guests coming for lunch, so I contemplated canceling. But everything had already been prepped therefore I chose to continue with the lunch. During this process, the enemy began to talk to me, "What kind of Mother are you anyway? Your son Is lying in the hospital with a broken neck, legs and debilitating injuries and you are carrying on as if all is all right!!"
I tried to shrug off that annoying voice but the more I tried, the more a feeling of anxiousness tried to invade my peace.

I quickly called my driver to take me to the hospital. You see, the enemy does not know it all! The lies he was feeding me about my son's condition led me to ask the right questions to find out the truth from the doctor when I eventually arrived at the hospital. I knew my husband had avoided giving me all the details of our son's condition. Besides he knew I was not in total agreement with our son's participation in the race and he didn't want me to be worried.

Arriving at the hospital, I found my son lying flat on his back, laughing and joking with the medical staff in his true nature. I glared at my husband, "Why did you allow this to happen? " I exclaimed, realizing that I was shouting, I lowered my voice.

The doctor heard the commotion and quickly came into the room to reassure me that all was well. There were no broken bones, thank God! They were keeping him on observation to check for a concussion. So far, no signs were present. Praise God!

My son was released after around 9 hours. He had no broken bones nor a concussion. I received so many messages from onlookers who had observed the accident. Some had taken videos and wanted me to see the stunt my son did resembling one of the famous 'Evel Knievel stunts' right out of the movies. I declined. They were all amazingly dumbfounded that my son had walked away completely unscathed! They all knew by the end of this event that I served the living and risen Christ!

The second part of the verse says God's peace will guard our hearts in Christ Jesus! Let us choose His peace and not to worry!

Pray:
Lord thank you that we can practice being thankful today, discard worry and wear your peace no matter what is going on in our lives. In Jesus Name, Amen!

Day 27 – Loose the Cords of Injustice

Isaiah 58:6-9b (NIV) :

"Is not this the kind of fasting I have chosen:
to loose the chains of injustice
    and untie the cords of the yoke,
to set the oppressed free
    and break every yoke?
[7] Is it not to share your food with the hungry
    and to provide the poor wanderer with shelter—
when you see the naked, to clothe them,
    and not to turn away from your own flesh and blood?
[8] Then your light will break forth like the dawn,

> and your healing will quickly appear;
> then your righteousness will go before you,
> and the glory of the Lord will be your rear guard.
> [9] Then you will call, and the Lord will answer;
> you will cry for help, and he will say: Here am I.
> b"If you do away with the yoke of oppression,
> with the pointing finger and malicious talk...

It is often after this halfway point that our resolve to fast becomes weakened. I invite you to cast your eyes upon Jesus the son of the Living God! You would think that out of all the people in the Bible he would not need to fast and pray but he did so more often and more frequently so that he could be in constant communion with the Father.

Right when some of us were tempted to be less stringent during this fast, we got a message from one of our diehard fasting sisters, Carol Smart, who has been doing an all liquid fast thus far and invited us to PUSH more in the Spirit (Carol Smart's testimony is included).

What have you given up so far? She challenged us to give up something else for 3 days! But I say not only 3 days but till we see the manifestation of what we have been seeking God to do! Remember fasting does not only move God rather it moves us closer to the reality of the Kingdom of God. It moves us towards believing in the supernatural and expecting it to take place in our lives.

The verses we read in Isaiah 58 tells us of the fast which MOST pleases the Lord. Does God want me to fast food? Yes, Jesus fasted more than anyone, we need to follow his example. But God also wants us to loose the cords of injustice, feed the hungry. He wants us to be mindful of how we fast.

Matthew 6:16 records: ¹⁶ "When you fast, do not look somber as the hypocrites do, for they disfigure their faces to show others they are fasting. Truly I tell you, they have received their reward in full. ¹⁷ But when you fast, put oil on your head and wash your face, ¹⁸ so that it will not be obvious to others that you are fasting, but only to your Father, who is unseen; and your Father, who sees what is done in secret, will reward you."

In the previous verses, Jesus also told them how to pray. Look at **Matthew 6:** ⁵ "And when you pray, do not be like the hypocrites, for they love to pray standing in the synagogues and on the street corners to be seen by others. Truly I tell you, they have received their reward in full. ⁶ But when you pray, go into your room, close the door and pray to your Father, who is unseen. Then your Father, who sees what is done in secret, will reward you."

Jesus did and spoke all those things to serve as an example for us. He often went away alone to commune with the Father. This is how he drew his strength through his relationship with Abba. This is so crucial for us to remember during our fasting. **Isaiah 58:9b,** says but when we fast, we need to do away with the yolk of oppression, malicious talk and pointing fingers. God wants us to get serious.

Drastic times call for drastic measures to uproot the enemy's territory for good! Are there cords of injustice to be uprooted or yokes to be destroyed in your life, or those of your family members, neighborhood, Church, city, town, country? God wants you to uproot those yokes and replace them with his perfect plans. The Bible says in **Job 22:28-30** ²⁸ "Thou shalt also decree a thing, and it shall be established unto thee: and the light shall shine upon thy ways."
What that signifies is that when you are in line with God's Word, you can SPEAK a thing, and GOD will bring it to pass. That is why it is crucial what we speak.

The Bible declares **in Isaiah 10:27** the yokes shall be destroyed because of the anointing! What is a yoke? In Bible days, yokes were placed on oxen in order to train them to carry heavy burdens. Problems sometimes may appear to be heavy burdens that weigh us down.

The Bible in **Matthew 11:28-30 (NIV)** states:
"28 Come to me, all you who are weary and burdened, and I will give you rest. 29 Take my yoke upon you and learn from me, for I am gentle and humble in heart, and you will find rest for your souls. 30 For my yoke is easy and my burden is light."

Jesus is saying to you today, His yoke is easy and his burden is light, rather take his yoke upon you and release the yokes of the enemy, generational yokes, bonds or sicknesses will be released right now in Jesus mighty name!

Pray: Stand during this prayer!
Father in the mighty name of Jesus, I release the burdens of (name them) off my family and my generation. I decree and declare that every yolk of addiction, infertility, divorce, porn, suicide (name them) are broken off my life and that of my posterity in Jesus mighty name!

Where there has been depression, I call forth joy, where there has been hatred, I choose love, where there has been sickness, I decree health in the mighty name of Jesus.

I banish all suicidal spirits off (name them) instead I proclaim life! I plead the blood of the Lamb of God over these yokes and burdens now, in Jesus Name.

I destroy every bond (you can actually use the cutting motion in the spirit) and I anoint with the oil of gladness (use anointing oil to anoint yourself and your home) in Jesus Mighty Name, Amen.

Day 28 – Spiritual Warfare/ Release Ungodly Thoughts

The Bible declares, our warfare is not against flesh and blood but principalities of evil in high places.

Oftentimes we see destruction in our lives seemingly caused by our loved ones or even our enemies or own flesh and blood, yet the root cause can sometimes be Satan and his cohorts.
Look at this exchange between Jesus and Peter when Peter seemed to be on the forefront of the support team of Jesus, yet he was totally against the will of the Father for Jesus' life.

Matthew 16:23 (NIV): "**23** Jesus turned and said to Peter, 'Get behind me, Satan! You are a stumbling block to me; you do not have in mind the concerns of God, but merely human concerns.'"

We are human but we do not wage war like humans do. James and John were nicknamed Sons of Thunder because they desired to destroy a Samaritan town that did not receive them.
Luke 9:54 (NIV): "**54** When the disciples James and John saw this, they asked, 'Lord, do you want us to call fire down from heaven to destroy them?'"
Jesus disagreed with them going on to the next village.

It states this in **2 Corinthians 10:3-5 (NLT):**
"**3** For though we live in the world, we do not wage war as the world does. **4** The weapons we fight with are not the weapons of the world. On the contrary, they have divine power to demolish strongholds. **5** We demolish arguments and every pretension that sets itself up against the knowledge of God, and we take captive every thought to make it obedient to Christ."

A Spiritual battle calls for Spiritual weapons. Spiritual warfare can involve a serious Battlefield of the Mind. Joyce Meyer's book 'Battlefield of the Mind', and 'Mind World' by Ron Carpenter are both exceptionally good spiritual resources if you would like to study more on this topic.

For Prayer purposes let us take captive those reasonings or thoughts that exalt themselves against The Word and KNOWLEDGE OF God. Let us look at Jesus' example during his 40 day fast when he hungered. When the enemy tempted him with food, His reply was **Matthew 5:3-4 (NIV):** "**3** The tempter came to him and said, 'If you are the Son of God, tell these stones to become bread.' **4** Jesus answered, 'It is written: "One does not live by bread alone, but by every word that proceeds from the mouth of God."'

He took captive the thought of hunger and applied God's Word. There was a time in my life as a young Christian that I had to take thoughts captive every few seconds as my mind ran rampant with the what if's and possibilities that could occur if......
I finally had to declare "thus saith the Lord!" Only THEN did I win the Spiritual Warfare in my Mind!

Pray like this, *place your hands on your head taking captive whatever thoughts are plaguing you right now. Get ready to bring those strongholds down in the name of Jesus. Declare the Living Word after having taken captive that/those thought(s).*

Day 29 – Be Prepared!

I left The Netherlands quite unexpectedly, although, I was totally prepared. You see, I was scheduled to travel out on the following

Monday; however, by the previous Thursday, my suitcase had been packed as well as all my spring cleaning concluded in my home there! On Friday, I decided to carry out some errands I planned to do the next day. I heard the Spirit say, "Don't put it off; do it now! Don't rest until you do" **Proverbs 6:4 (NLT).**

I even did a little last-minute shopping, cooked some of my youngest's (Danielle) favorite dishes to freeze before retiring to bed at around 1 AM. The airline had advised to check on their App 72 hours prior to flying to see if any changes to the flight had been made. Therefore, when I checked at 1 AM and saw that it was suggested I fly out in a few hours, I was a little surprised, but I had no need for panic. I was ready! I calmly made the necessary arrangements/booked taxi, slept for a couple of hours waking up 1 minute before my alarm sounded!

Will you be ready before the trumpet sounds? Would you have made all preparations and put your life in order?

So, the Lord says, will be the "Parousia," (Greek word meaning presence or official visit) Second Coming as a thief in the night. Jesus Christ will come surreptitiously without warning, and all Believers will be raptured from the earth.

He plainly describes the event in **Matthew 24: 40-41 (NIV):** "**40** Then two men will be in the field; one is taken, and one is left. **41** Two women will be grinding with a hand mill; one will be taken and the other left." This event is referred to as the rapture.

Many have had dreams of the Second Coming of Jesus Christ, I have not. One of my dear friends Amelie, who is from Gabon, told me she had attended a Powerful Spiritual Revival in Nigeria along with hundreds of other people. That night she dreamed of the rapture! She perceived that only people who were "light in spirit" those who had given their burdens and sins to the Lord would be taken up with Him!

During a particularly fiery revival involving an African Pastor in Alabama, a friend's husband went to bed as normal but awoke disoriented and terrified because he could not find his wife in the house and thought the rapture had taken place! He was aware of the Second Coming of Jesus Christ but had not made proper preparations for the Lord's return. He was doing all the "Churchy" things, but his heart was not completely devoted to the Lord. This experience had a profound impact on his life resulting in a 180 degree turn around!

Although I've never dreamed about the rapture, my recent travel experience coupled with the signs of the times reinforced a valuable truth, which happens to be the Boy and Girl Scout Troops' motto "Be Prepared" (I learned this from my grandson being a boy scout).

It states in **Matthew 24:42-44 NKJV:** "**42**Watch therefore, for you do not know on what day your Lord is coming. **43** But know this, that if the householder had known in what part of the night the thief was coming, he would have watched and would not have let his house be broken into. **44** Therefore, you must be ready; for the son of man is coming at an hour you do not expect."

Jesus is surely coming back for His GLORIOUS Church without a spot or a wrinkle. Therefore, be on guard! There is a song the choir sings at my Beloved Church in Alabama. The first stanza reads:

I Shall Wear a Crown
Watch ye, therefore, you know not the day
When the Lord shall call your soul away
If you labor, strivin' for the right
You shall wear a robe and crown

Let us Pray:
Heavenly Father, I want to be ready when you come back. Help me to release heavy burdens and sins that weigh me down! Holy Spirit, would you prepare me for this great and awesome day? I do not want to be left behind but I want to be prepared for your glorious Second Coming! In Jesus Name, Amen.

Day 30 – Emmanuel is with Us

This is the Word the Lord gave me at the end of 2019. With hesitation, I included it in my New Year's Greetings to many of you.

I discussed it during our Christmas Day Devotional time with my family and friends Carol and Stephen Smart. I did not have a lot of commentary to say because frankly, I didn't know at the time what type of war was coming, I only knew I felt the Lord telling me to announce it and by doing so in the time of trials, I would reassure all that Emmanuel is with us!

I prefer to be the bearer of Good news not Bad News especially at the beginning of a year that everyone was proclaiming would be 20/20 in every arena.

Yet the Lord spoke it so clearly and so precisely that I had no other choice but to obey.
This Word brought a great source of comfort to me in an odd sort of way just by knowing that no matter what we would have to face, Emmanuel is with us.

Let us first read **Isaiah 8:9-10 in the King James Version**.

Isaiah 8:9-10 (KJV):
"**9** Associate yourselves, O ye people, and ye shall be broken in pieces; and give ear, all ye of far countries: gird yourselves, and ye shall be broken in pieces; gird yourselves, and ye shall be broken in pieces. **10** Take counsel together, and it shall come to naught; speak the word, and it shall not stand: for God is with us."

This Word was spoken to Syria, Israel and Judah because of their disobedience. It could represent all the nations of the earth today. I like this commentary from Enduring Word.
I put my thoughts in parenthesis bold and italicized for comparison of modern world events in real time.

"Gird yourselves, but be broken in pieces… speak the word, but it will not stand, for God *(**Emmanuel**)* is with us: The victims of this Assyrian invasion *(**Coronavirus invasion against the entire world**)* could prepare for the invasion all they wanted *(**gird yourselves**)*. But all their preparation would not protect them *(**but be broken in pieces**)*. They could take counsel together, but it will come to nothing *(**The nations of the world are frantically seeking solutions**)*. All their plans and words and ideas will not stand, for God is with us. God's will would prevail, despite all the plans and preparations Syria, Israel, and Judah *(**the entire world**)* might make against it."

Dearly Beloved, we have the assurance of Emmanuel being with us and Hallelujah, that is enough, Selah! He is the Mighty one in this Battle, He is Jehovah-Rophe our Healer, the government is on his shoulders.
Isaiah 9:6 (NIV) reads:
"For to us a child is born, to us a son is given, and the government will be on his shoulders. And he will be called Wonderful Counselor, Mighty God, Everlasting Father, Prince of Peace."

The Lord promises when we keep our eyes fixated upon Him (not news 24/7), we will be kept in perfect peace **(Isaiah 26:3)**. I maintain my belief and assurance that as suddenly as this insidious disease (demonic infestation) has swept down upon us, it will also vanish because our Almighty God will snuff it out! We must pray fervently in one accord!

Let us end by reading **Isaiah 8:7b-14** in the New Living Translation.

Isaiah 8:7b-14 (NLT):
7b "This will overflow all its channels **8** and sweep into Judah until it is chin deep. It will spread its wings, submerging your land from one end to the other, O Immanuel.
9 "Huddle together, you nations, and be terrified. Listen, all you distant lands. Prepare for battle, but you will be crushed! Yes, prepare for battle, but you will be crushed! **10** Call your councils of war, but they will be worthless. Develop your strategies, but they will not succeed. For God is with us**.**"

A Call to Trust the Lord
11 The Lord has given me a strong warning not to think like everyone else does. He said,
12 'Don't call everything a conspiracy, like they do, and don't live in dread of what frightens them. **13** Make the Lord of Heaven's Armies holy in your life. He is the one you should fear. He is the one who should make you tremble. **14** He will keep you safe.'"

Pray:
Lord your Holy Word declares, "So shall they fear the name of the LORD from the west, And His glory from the rising of the sun. When the enemy comes in like a flood, The Spirit of the LORD will lift up a standard against him." **Isaiah 59:19 (KJV).**

Jehovah Nissi, You alone are our banner in this unseen war. The enemy has swept down upon the nations as a mighty flood! But O LORD OUR GOD, raise your standard against the enemy! Our hope and confidence are in you, Abba. You have given us Emmanuel, the Governments of this world will be upon his shoulders, come to our aid, O Lord. For you have promised to heal. In Jesus Mighty Name, Amen.

Reflections

_____

_____

_____

_____

_____

_____

_____

_____

_____

_____

_____

_____

For in Him we live and move and have our being. As some of your own poets have said, "We are his offspring."

Acts 17:28 NIV

Day 31 – Release Restoration over the Nations

Hosea 6:1-3 (NIV):
"**1** Come, let us return to the Lord. He has torn us to pieces but he will heal us; he has injured us but he will bind up our wounds. **2** After two days he will revive us; on the third day he will restore us, that we may live in his presence. **3** Let us acknowledge the Lord; let us press on to acknowledge him. As surely as the sun rises, he will appear; he will come to us like the winter rains, like the spring rains that water the earth."

What beautiful promises of restoration from the Lord! Your head must be reeling with questions such as 'How will you do it Lord'? 'When will the plague stop'? 'What do I need to do to prevent destruction from coming near my dwelling'?

2 Peter 3:8 (ESV): states:
"**8** But do not overlook this one fact, beloved, that with the Lord one day is as a thousand years, and a thousand years as one day."
Simply put, God's timeline is different from ours.

Isaiah 55:8 (NLT) sums it all up by God telling us precisely:
"My thoughts are nothing like your thoughts," says the LORD. "And my ways are far beyond anything you could imagine."

- He uses Moses' rod to open the Red Sea.
- He chooses a prostitute to hide the spies who went to spy out Jericho and we later find Rahab in the genealogy of Jesus!
- He rebukes Balaam the prophet using a donkey to speak to him!
- He uses a small boy David to kill Goliath, a giant.

- He uses 5 loaves and 2 fish to feed 5000 men (that does not include women and children).
- He turns water into wine.
- He selects a young virgin girl, Mary, to bring Jesus into the world!

Clearly His ways are higher than ours nor can we fathom, comprehend, imitate, imagine the ways of Almighty God!

The text calls for repentance as well as an invitation for healing. The Lord wants to bring both Revival in two days and Restoration to his people on the third.

Understanding that Jesus himself came up out of the grave on the third day gives us a hint of the magnitude of restoration Abba wants to bestow upon us!
The text presupposes that the calamity was from the Lord equally the restoration and revival will be from God. The requirement? Repentance. Turn from our wicked ways so our land can be healed.

Let us as one voice acknowledge and call upon the name of the Lord. He promises to come as surely as the sun rises in the morning. He will come to us like the winter's rain, like the spring rain washes the earth. Rain signifies a Spiritual blessing, salvation for the nations.

The Lord wants us to live in His presence. The Psalmist rejoices in **Psalms 16:11 (NIV):** "You make known to me the path of life; you will fill me with joy in your presence, with eternal pleasures at your right hand."

Today, I want each of us to 'Stand in the Gap for a nation' of the world that has been afflicted and cry out on behalf of that nation. Repent on behalf of the Head of State, Cabinet Members, Nationals.

Ask the Lord to cleanse the land from this insidious demonic force with the blood that flows from Calvary's stream.

On Calvry's hill of sorrow
Where sin's demands were paid,
And rays of hope for tomorrow
Across our path were laid.
I see a crimson stream of blood,
It flows from Calvary,
Its waves which reach the throne of God,
Are sweeping over me.

My Soul Longs for You by Jesus Culture Bethel Music

https://youtu.be/OUJQx_JmtVA

Day 32 – Released from my Mind Prison!

Learning about how the ex-President of South Africa, Nelson Mandela spent 27 years wrongfully in Prison was amazing to me. Though I have visited his beloved country many times, I have never had the opportunity to visit his jail cell on Robben Island.

Many Heads of State and tourists have gone to gaze upon the simple cell in wonder marveling over the magnitude of a man who lived there. There was no magic in Nelson Mandela's making, just as there was none in Joseph's imprisonment in Egypt or Jesus' who broke out of the grave on Easter Sunday! I dare not compare these men to the latter however I must say the Battlefield was fought in the Mind!

In the case of Nelson Mandela, it was 'His Long Walk to Freedom" which subsequently set his people free. Nelson Mandela emerged from a 27-year unlawful jail sentence with no bitterness despite the wrong afflicted upon him. He was transformed from hating his enemy to developing character traits which led him to becoming one of the most Beloved leaders not only of South Africa but the entire world!

With Joseph, it was his fear of the Lord's commandments which landed him in prison in the first place! Then the gift the Lord placed inside of him developed and was activated during his prison days, eventually bringing him from the pit, to Potiphar's house, his integrity put him in prison, but his dream interpretation took him to the Palace!

Jesus fought his Battlefield of the mind in the garden of Gethsemane. He subdued his flesh and made the ultimate sacrifice for all of humanity!

Look at **Luke 22:41-44 (ESV):** "**41** And he withdrew from them about a stone's throw, and knelt down and prayed, **42** saying, "Father, if you are willing, remove this cup from me. Nevertheless, not my will, but yours, be done." **43** And there appeared to him an angel from heaven, strengthening him. **44** And being in agony he prayed more earnestly; and his sweat became like great drops of blood falling down to the ground."

Jesus Christ experienced hematohidrosis while praying in the garden of Gethsemane before his crucifixion as mentioned in the Defenders Bible by Physician Luke. Hematohidrosis is a rare condition in which a human being sweats blood.

Jesus wrestled with his flesh but made up his mind to do His Father's will. Jesus cried out "NOT MY WILL, FATHER, BUT YOUR WILL BE DONE!" The grave could not hold him because his mind was made up!

Until you figure out what the fight is all about, you can win the battle but lose the fight! You see the Battlefield is in the Mind! There are no boundaries when it comes to what the mind can do! You can imprison ones' body but when your mind is free, life is best lived!

The Bible declares in **Isaiah 61:1a (NIV):** "**1a** The Spirit of the Sovereign LORD is on me, because the LORD has anointed me to proclaim good news to the poor. He has sent me to bind up the brokenhearted, to proclaim freedom for the captives and release from darkness for the prisoners..."

If you are feeling oppressed or depressed in your mind, Jesus has come to set you free. If you are having suicidal thoughts, the price of your freedom is in a drop of blood from our Savior Jesus Christ. He has come to release captives from their dark prisons. He wants to set you free with a Word today!
Look at this verse of scripture:
Psalms 34:6 (KJV) proclaims: "This poor man cried, and the LORD heard him, and saved him out of all his troubles."

This following Psalm is power packed with imagery of impenetrable bars of brass and iron, yet the power of God broke down the brass door and cut off the bars of iron. Nothing is too hard for God! He is ready to release you from your High Security Prison right now!

Psalms 107:14-16; 20 (KJV) reads:
14 He brought them out of darkness and the shadow of death and brake their bands in sunder. **15** Oh that men would praise the Lord for his goodness, and for his wonderful works to the children of men! **16** For he hath broken the gates of brass and cut the bars of iron in sunder.
20 He sent his word, and healed them, and delivered them from their destructions."

God can deliver you from your prison cell today! Get this, Paul and Silas were doing the praying and singing but the bands of every man were loosed! Released by the hand of Almighty God! This is what it states in:

Acts 16:25-25 (KJV): "**25** And at midnight Paul and Silas prayed, and sang praises unto God: and the prisoners heard them.**26** And suddenly there was a great earthquake, so that the foundations of the prison were shaken: and immediately all the doors were opened, and every one's bands were loosed."

Hallelujah! May the foundations of your Mind Prison, Addiction Prison, Physical Prison be shaken by an earthquake today! May you go free in Jesus Name!

Decreeing today Father that as we sing, pray and magnify your name, you will send an earthquake to release every prisoner and set them free in Jesus name! Amen.

Pray like this:
Lay your hands upon your head, Father in the name of Jesus, I release myself from the prison of oppression, depression, suicidal thoughts and spiritual unrest! As I praise you right now, these bands and shackles shall fall off me and I shall be set free, in Jesus Mighty Name, Amen!

No Longer Slaves by Jonathan David & Melissa Helser

https://youtu.be/f8TkUMJtK5k

Day 33 – The Crown of Thorns

The Covid-19, as the disease has been named by WHO, falls under a larger umbrella of Coronaviruses. Coronaviruses derive their name from the fact that under electron microscopic examination, each virion is surrounded by a "corona", halo. The name Corona itself means crown. Covid-19 not having originated from humans, is difficult to contain because we have virtually no immunity. Doctors are working frantically for a vaccine but in the meanwhile, it has been recommended to take social distancing seriously by staying in one's home.

While meditating about this peculiar virus, I was reassured of a few things. First, the name.

Philippians 2:9-10 (KJV) declares:
"**9** Wherefore God also hath highly exalted him, and given him a name which is above every name: **10** That at the name of Jesus every knee should bow, of things in heaven, and things in earth, and things under the earth;"

Covid-19 has a name, it now resides here on earth therefore at the name of Jesus it shall bow! Hallelujah, to the glory of God! Let us proclaim that in ONE ACCORD!

Next, its appearance is like a crown. I searched the Bible finding over 66 references to crowns in 28 books but decided only to share a few here to support my point.

Psalms 65:11 (NLT) indicates this:
"**11** You crown the year with a bountiful harvest; even the hard pathways overflow with abundance."

The Lord of the Harvest has announced the harvest is ripe! Even 'the hard pathways', rather some who are agnostics and atheists will be baffled at the state of this present world and desire to turn to the Lord. God wants to get the attention of the world to look to HIM, the only one with a solution to this pandemic. God wants to save physically and spiritually! What a beautiful assurance! Our job is to help reach the lost on our pathway.

Do not be shy about bringing Jesus into the conversation when you are discussing this Pandemic.

The Lord says in **Psalms 81:10 (NIV)**:
"Open your mouth wide, I will fill it." Again, in **Luke 12:12** the Holy Spirit reassures you that he will give you the right thing to say at the right time. You cannot get it wrong Believer when you are applying God's Word! The Bible declares that his Word will not return void, it will accomplish its purpose **Isaiah 55:11**. Therefore, it is for you to proclaim, and the Holy Spirit to accomplish!

You see Satan, a created being, wanted to exalt his throne over the Creator and was hurled out of heaven to earth! Read **Isaiah 14:13a (NIV)**: "You said in your heart, 'I will ascend to the heavens; I will raise my throne above the stars of God...'"

A thorough read of **Ezekiel 28** and **Isaiah 14** teaches us what a beautiful but prideful creature Satan really was. Light radiated from his being. He was exquisitely dressed, was a singer/worshiper who had more moves than the King of Pop himself! Yet, he desired to raise his throne above God's and was hurled from heaven to earth where man resides. He has waged war with Mankind since the Garden of Eden. His desire is to remove our crowns since he has none! He does not want us in eternity with Jesus. Do not be deceived brethren! His plan is deceitful, and Satan will stop at nothing to destroy Mankind.

In **Job 2:6-7 (NIV)**, it is clear when Satan appeared before God along with the Holy angels and pin-pointed the man Job because of his uprightness and dedication to God. Satan was determined to destroy Job's life and cause him to curse God. The verses read:

6 "'Very well,' said the LORD to Satan. 'He is in your hands, but you must spare his life' **7** So Satan went out from the presence of the Lord and infected Job with terrible boils from the soles of his feet to the crown of his head.

Satan was determined to remove Job's crown! Look what it states in **Revelation 2:10 (MSG):**
10 "Fear nothing in the things you're about to suffer—but stay on guard! Fear nothing! The Devil is about to throw you in jail for a time of testing—ten days. It won't last forever.
Don't quit, even if it costs you your life. Stay there believing. I have a Life-Crown sized and ready for you."

The next thing I want you to notice about 'crown' is that the Lord declares he is the one who redeems your life from the pit and crowns you with love and compassion **Psalm 103:4.**
Satan is a counterfeit! He knows what crown denotes in the political sense as well as the spiritual. He wishes to remove the crown of love and compassion God has given to us and place instead upon our heads a crown of deceit, disease or death.

From the beginning, he sought to usurp the authority of the Father and was kicked out of heaven onto the earth waging war with human beings. Notice the virus is not from a human source.

Revelation 12:7-12 (AMP):
The Angel, Michael
7 And war broke out in heaven, Michael [the archangel] and his angels waging war with the dragon. The dragon and his angels fought, **8** but they were not strong enough *and* did not prevail, and there was no longer a place found for them in heaven. **9** And the great dragon was thrown down, the age-old serpent who is called the devil and Satan, he who *continually* deceives *and* seduces the entire inhabited world; he was thrown down to the earth, and his

angels were thrown down with him. **10** Then I heard a loud voice in heaven, saying,
"Now the salvation, and the power, and the kingdom (dominion, reign) of our God, and the authority of His Christ have come; for the accuser of our [believing] brothers and sisters has been thrown down [at last], he who accuses them *and* keeps bringing charges [of sinful behavior] against them before our God day and night. **11** And they overcame *and* conquered him because of the blood of the Lamb and because of the word of their testimony, for they did not love their life *and* renounce their faith even when faced with death. **12** Therefore rejoice, O heavens and you who dwell in them [in the presence of God]. Woe to the earth and the sea, because the devil has come down to you in great wrath, knowing that he has *only* a short time [remaining]!"

Verse 11 states, "And they overcame and conquered Satan by the blood of the lamb and the word of our testimony. The verse goes on to say, "for they did not love their life *and* renounce their faith even when faced with death."

Beloved, I foresee that these are just the beginning of birth pains and there are perilous times ahead, but Emmanuel is with us! I predict the Lord will take some Saints home to prevent their suffering. We can still have hope in the Glorious Second Coming of our Lord Jesus Christ when we have been redeemed and our names are written in the book of life! What a magnificent truth and confidence in our Lord, The Prince of Peace.

It reads here in **John 19:5 (AMP)**:
"Then came Jesus forth, wearing the crown of thorns, and the purple robe. And [Pilate] saith unto them, Behold the man!"
According to Wikipedia there are around 500 Relics of the 'crown of thorns', bought by Louis IX from Baldwin II. It was preserved at the

Notre-Dame de Paris until 15 April 2019, when it was rescued from a fire at the cathedral.

Pilate in mockery called Jesus a King! And He was! He wore the crown of thorns and conquered death forever upon the cross of Golgotha. I want to propose to you Covi-19 was destroyed upon the cross of Golgotha! Jesus said, "It is finished", and so it shall be! **John 19:30 (NIV).**

Pray:
Lord Jesus, you wore a crown of thorns, you conquered sickness and death upon the cross. Covid-19 has been conquered in Jesus Name. Every knee shall bow at the name of Jesus, Covid-19 shall bow in Jesus Name. We pray for the VIP's who have contracted the illness as well as the common folk. You love us all Father and your explicit desire is not that we perish. Protect us o Lord, from the evil One. Help us to withstand unto the end O Lord, I do not want to forfeit my crown of life prepared for me because my name has been written in the book of Life in Jesus Mighty Name, Amen!

Day 34 – The Branch

Yesterday while meditating about this peculiar virus which has already begun to mutate, I could see it as if it were an invisible army invading the world scene. Like a Terrorist of some sort. Then I remembered before leaving Kuala Lumpur, Malaysia a few years ago, I had had a dream of a seemingly invisible war swirling around in the wind like leaves but though I saw it as being a war, I didn't see any artillery such as weapons of warfare. Though I had this dream in Malaysia, I saw myself in the USA.

Then again when I left Holland returning to the USA in December 2018, the Firenight's Team prayed for me and much had to do with 'war' and intercessory prayer.

Again in December of 2019, the Lord spoke to me from **Isaiah 8: 9-10 and 16 (NIV):** "**9** Raise the war cry you nations, and be shattered! Listen, all you distant lands. Prepare for battle, and be shattered! Prepare for battle, and be shattered! **10** Devise your strategy, but it will be thwarted; propose your plan, but it will not stand, for God is with us. **16** Bind up this testimony of warning and seal up God's instruction among my disciples."

As an intercessor or a Prophetess, the Lord may give you a dream or a revelation and you understand in part (see **1 Corinthians 13:9**).

Habakkuk 2:2 tells us to write the vision down because it will surely come to pass. While writing this Devotional, the Lord brought that dream back to my memory.

Psalms 8 is a beautiful Psalm. **Verses 4 a, 5 read**:
"**4** what is mankind that you are mindful of them, human beings that you care for them? **5** You have made them a little lower than the angels and crowned them with glory and honor." David continues in this Psalm to speak of the authority God gave us in the Garden of Eden.

As we know, Adam handed this authority over to Satan. Therefore, Satan is operating legally upon this earth, please understand that when you pray. BUT Jesus crowned in all his glory took back this authority when he died upon the cross and returned it to us!

He says in **Matthew 16:19 (NIV):** "I will give you the keys of the Kingdom of heaven. Whatever you bind on earth will be bound in heaven, and whatever you loose on earth will be loosed in heaven. "

Jesus also said in **Luke 10:18-20 (NIV):**
"**18** He replied, 'I saw Satan fall like lightning from heaven. **19** I have given you authority to trample on snakes and scorpions and to overcome all the power of the enemy; nothing will harm you. **20** However, do not rejoice that the spirits submit to you, but rejoice that your names are written in heaven.'"

Jesus has reminded us of the power he has returned to us but also that our names are written in the Book of Life. Jesus is letting us know our ultimate goal is to make heaven! Our Ministry or Life's Purpose should never overshadow our "Eternal Crown in Glory"! Our salvation cost Jesus his life!

Yet the enemy is relentless in his pursuit to bring us to naught. Let us see what happened to Joshua.

Zechariah 3:1-10(NIV):
"**1** Then he showed me Joshua the high priest standing before the angel of the Lord, and Satan standing at his right side to accuse him. **2** The Lord said to Satan, 'The Lord rebuke you, Satan! The Lord, who has chosen Jerusalem, rebuke you! Is not this man a burning stick snatched from the fire?' **3** Now Joshua was dressed in filthy clothes as he stood before the angel. **4** The angel said to those who were standing before him, 'Take off his filthy clothes.'
Then he said to Joshua, 'See, I have taken away your sin, and I will put fine garments on you.' **5** Then I said, 'Put a clean turban on his head.' So, they put a clean turban on his head and clothed him, while the angel of the Lord stood by."
Joshua was a priest but represented Jerusalem, a man of God yet the enemy came against him mightily. The filthy clothes he was wearing represented the iniquity in the land and the change to fine robes was symbolic of Jerusalem's restoration.

"**6** The angel of the Lord gave this charge to Joshua: **7** 'This is what the Lord Almighty says: 'If you will walk in obedience to me and keep my requirements, then you will govern my house and have charge of my courts, and I will give you a place among these standing here. **8** Listen, High Priest Joshua, you and your associates seated before you, who are men symbolic of things to come: I am going to bring my servant, the Branch. **9** See, the stone I have set in front of Joshua! There are seven eyes on that one stone, and I will engrave an inscription on it,' says the Lord Almighty, 'and I will remove the sin of this land in a single day. **10** In that day each of you will invite your neighbor to sit under your vine and fig tree,' declares the Lord Almighty.'"

Hallelujah! Did you see what I saw while reading this? First the Lord re-establishes Joshua in his role as priest complete with fine garments and a lovely turban (representing crown for me), tells Joshua if he walks in obedience, he will govern his house (Church). The Lord continues to say in verse 8 Joshua and his associates are symbolic of things to come! Now I have got your attention! Verse 9 speaks of Jesus being the Branch and the solid stone foundation sat before Joshua (Jerusalem). The foundation or houses of worship such as the Church or Jewish Temple in this case. The eye is a sign of Providence and the number 7 the sign of perfection. The Church of Jesus Christ and its Believers are only made perfect through Jehovah Tsidkenu, God our Righteousness.

I would like to address your attention to verse 9b "and I will remove the sin of this land in a single day". In this instance, The "one day" of its removal is primarily the day of national atonement celebrated after the completion of the temple Leviticus **23:27** on the tenth day of the seventh month. But what if, just what if the Lord chose to remove the sin of the lands of the entire world in one day and wipe out this current plague in 2020?

Isaiah 14:26-27 (NIV) declares:
"**26** This is the plan determined for the whole world; this is the hand stretched out over all nations. **27** For the Lord Almighty has purposed, and who can thwart him? His hand is stretched out, and who can turn it back?"

Let us Pray:
Father in the mighty name of Jesus, just as you took away the iniquity of Jerusalem, wiped it all out and re-established your nation in one day, we beseech you O Lord to do it for us. Lord, would you remove the Silent Killer Plague that has invaded the entire world? Would you restore the nations, Jehovah Tsidkenu, God our Righteousness? The Enemy has desired to sift us like wheat but O Lord, your 7 eyes are roving to and fro over the nations. You have seen the wickedness poured out upon us, yet in a single day, you can remove the sin of all the nations of the earth.

We have no other recourse Abba Father, except to turn to you with our petition today. Without your intervention, the entire world would be lost, we implore your grace and loving kindness Father. We are undeserving just as Jerusalem was, yet you showed mercy. In Jesus Mighty Name, Amen!

Research Reference: Bible Study Tools

Reflections

_____

_____

_____

Testimony | Daria Morris

Dearest Sister,

Thank you again for sowing into me and subsequently sowing into my family and friends. During the study "Release the Dove" I often fought with myself about whether or not I should be a part of the group. But every week, something pulled me back in. By week 3, I couldn't imagine my Tuesdays without it! On multiple occasions, the study would either answer questions that I had been contemplating during the week or give me Biblical perspective on something that I would face soon after. It was absolutely Spirit filled! There were quite a few chains that were broken during our time together. However, I believe the biggest breakthrough came after all the other very important breakthroughs during the study. It occurred during the time of fasting...

For at least two years I have been searching within myself and seeking God to reveal to me what it was in my spirit that I held against my mother. I have always loved her dearly. I have always respected her immensely (except for my very rebellious senior year of high school). But, in the past few years there was "something". I couldn't put my finger on it. I would be angry with her and it would be reflected in my tone towards her. I would judge her in my mind. It was torture and I couldn't understand why!

One morning during the time of fasting I was in prayer, the Lord revealed to me that I was angry with her for "allowing" herself to get sick. For years she struggled with diabetes and high blood pressure. A few years ago, she was diagnosed with chronic kidney disease. He revealed to me that I was angry with her because she didn't do what I felt in my mind was enough to combat the diseases. He showed me that I had to forgive her and I had to forgive myself for judging her so harshly. He showed me that she did what she could with what she had at the time. It was that simple.

Warning: the rest is graphic

During this time, I was experiencing my monthly cycle. When I stood up from praying, there was a rush of fluids unlike any that I can ever recall having. It was like a release. I knew it was a release in the spirit that was manifesting physically. Later that day, I spoke to my mom and made just a very casual mention of the mess. I didn't mention my revelation at all. I told her I suspected it may have just been that I was standing and the pressure caused the release.

I'm a bit ashamed as I downplayed my experience. But she asked me if I thought that was all that it was. She went on to tell me that she had gone to the restroom and when she wiped she saw blood. But when she looked again, there was no blood. She is about 15 years into menopause, so she didn't have any blood there. But her statement was confirmation to me that the Lord had in fact released me from the bondage of judgement and fear of losing my mom due to her chronic illnesses.

Reflections

_____

_____

_____

Day 35 – The Finest Hour of Christ's Glorious Church

I have been a blessed participant in revivals held around the world with well-known evangelists such as Reinhard Bonnke, Benny Hinn, Randy Clark, Bill Johnson and Morris Cerullo.

I have had the distinct pleasure of working many years with Double Portion's Evangelist Envoy Sarah Banks who may not have been known around the world but nevertheless was a Giant in the faith. I have been privy to host many Pastors from African countries, USA, Europe who were no doubt in the same caliber as the Lord's Generals, top men of God, powerful in Word and Ministry.

Both my husband and I have been honored time and time again by being in their presence. We have seen miracles that were astonishing, yet the Lord declares there is a Greater Works Ministry in this latter day. I have such a feeling of expectancy having only seen a taste of what God has prepared for his glorious Church.

I remember Morris Cerullo saying years ago, as surely as the world advances in technology, the Church would also see an advancement in the Spiritual. It is so close in fact, I believe we are now living in those days. This will be the latter dispensation whereby men and women of God will have such miraculous occurrences happen seemingly without any need to fast.

Reinhard Bonnke used to say for one hour of ministry you needed to pray for 2 hours, yet I believe with this Greater Works Ministry on the Horizon, we will see the miraculous occur daily! This will not only take place in Church but in the marketplace, on the streets, in restaurants or on your job.

The Glorious Church will now be seen more on a global level, not just confined to buildings made by hands. It will be the undeniable divine finger of God!

In the Bible where Jesus fed the 5000 with 5 loaves and 2 fish, he later taught on being the bread of life. Every miracle done was strategic for people to believe in the Messiah. Today will be no different. Abba is desiring to reap a soul harvest at the hands of ordinary men and women such as ourselves.

Look what it states here in **John 14:12 (NIV):**
"Very truly I tell you, whoever believes in me will do the works I have been doing, and they will do even greater things than these, because I am going to the Father."
There will be a need to think of the Church as the Kingdom of God and not just a building whereby people will meet. There will be a great cry for holiness and consecration from the Father. He is seeking a church without a spot or wrinkle.

Ephesians 5:27 (NIV) declares:
"27 and to present her to himself as a radiant church, without stain or wrinkle or any other blemish, but holy and blameless."

Revelation 3: (NIV) warns:
"**11** I am coming soon. Hold on to what you have, so that no one will take your crown."
To the Church of Laodicea, the Lord said,
"**15** I know your deeds, that you are neither cold nor hot. I wish you were either one or the other! **16** So, because you are lukewarm—neither hot nor cold—I am about to spit you out of my mouth."

Let us resolve to be on fire for Jesus under every circumstance. Let us rid ourselves of any besetting sins.

Hebrews 12:1a (KJV) says:
"Wherefore seeing we also are compassed about with so great a cloud of witnesses, let us lay aside every weight, and the sin which doth so easily beset us, and let us run with patience the race that is set before us,"

A besetting sin is one to which on account of our constitution, or circumstance or both, we are peculiarly exposed, and into which we most easily and most frequently fall. In the life of every individual, there is a "besetting" sin that can tower like a mountain between the individual and God (ref. dailywritingtip.com).

The very next verse, **Hebrews 12:2** tells us how best to run this race:
"**2** Looking unto Jesus the author and finisher of our faith, who for the joy that was set before him endured the cross, despising the shame, and is set down at the right hand of the throne of God."

Beloved, we need to look unto Jesus. He took our sin upon the cross. He is the Author of our lives. He knows the first chapter and the last page. We only need to put our trust in God.

In **John 17:20-21 (ESV)** Jesus Prays for us:
"**20** I do not ask for these only, but also for those who will believe in me through their word, **21** that they may all be one, just as you, Father, are in me, and I in you, that they also may be in us, so that the world may believe that you have sent me."

Jesus said to Peter in **Matthew 16:18 (NIV):**
"**18** And I tell you that you are Peter, and on this rock, I will build My church, and the gates of Hades will not prevail against it."

Rest assured dear One, the Glorious Church of Jesus Christ, meaning the Body of Christ is built on a solid foundation and entering its finest hour. I am not referring to a certain denomination or building, rather a genuine child of God who has given over the reins of his or her life to Jesus Christ. If you have not done this Beloved, the Bible states in **Romans 10:9 (NIV) :** "If you declare with your mouth, "Jesus is Lord," and believe in your heart that God raised him from the dead, you will be saved."

Pray:
Lord, you have declared there is a finer hour for your Glorious Bride, the Church. There is a Greater Works Ministry you wish to bestow upon your people. I declare with my mouth that Jesus is Lord and I believe in my heart that God you raised Jesus from the dead. I confess my sins to you and ask for forgiveness. You are coming back for a Church without a spot or a wrinkle. Purify me, O God so that I may go forth in your strength and power to work the works of God. In Jesus Mighty Name, Amen.

Sinach - I know who I am

https://youtu.be/frtZ4XfoXxM

Reflections

_____

_____

_____

_____

_____

Reflections

Lift up your heads, you gates; be lifted up, you ancient doors, that the King of glory may come in.

Psalms 24:7 NIV

Day 36 – Those who Dream!

Psalms 126:1
A song of ascents. When the LORD restored the fortunes of Zion, we were like those who dreamed.

This Psalm echoed in my spirit after I had attended a Women's Conference in Nigeria. I had been a guest speaker as well as the Mistress of Ceremony for the event. I had been living in The Hague as well as working full-time when I received the invite to travel for the conference.

It is a well-known fact that I seldom sleep on flights especially when I have meetings planned. I usually study the Word and prepare during the flight. This occasion was no different.

The organizer (who is one of my best friends and a leading doctor in Lagos) and I sat in the car outside the event. She was holding a small box of scriptures which contained promises from the Bible.

She held her precious commodity tight to her bosom and said in a raspy voice, "Let's choose a promise before the conference begins," she suggested.
"Good idea," I replied thinking, I needed all the blessings I could get from the Lord. Not only was I jet-lagged but also felt ill prepared for this event.

Arriving at the venue, the place was jam packed. Dr. Bero asked my opinion on the order of the service. Left up to me, no dinner would have been served; however, the plan was already set in place. I suggested we have dinner near the end of the event to allow people to focus on the Spiritual (food), Word of God rather than the physical.

The fire of the Holy Spirit was present. From the moment I introduced the first speaker, she took the microphone and prophesied to me that I would minister to people of all different nationalities yellow, white, black etc. I marveled at her words because "yellow" referred to Asians. I had always had a desire to live in Asia. My husband had thought it an impossibility due to job complications or technicalities, yet and still I had secretly prayed to move there knowing God could cut all the red tape.

I anticipated this would be a Spirit filled evening. The atmosphere was charged and surprisingly, the fatigue I previously felt seemingly vanished into thin air upon entrance into the venue. I could sense the place had been bathed in prayers as the presence of God was tangible. Every Speaker thereafter ministered in the exact same vein gaining momentum with each Minister.

I was the last to speak therefore no formal introduction was needed. As the Lord would have it, prophecy and words of knowledge spilled forth. I singled out one woman who I will refer to as Faith and told her she would have a child. I found out much later this was a medical impossibility. Not only was Faith 49 years of age but she had been married for almost 15 years and had never been pregnant nor had a late cycle! I shook my head wondering what possessed me to say those words to her.

I focused my attention back to Faith and her husband who were sitting across from me after the service. They had sought me out for additional prayers. Suddenly, I remembered the promise I had randomly chosen from the little box Dr Bero had held so tight prior to the event!
To my closest recollection the scripture was either **Matthew 24: 35 (NIV):** "Heaven and earth will pass away, but my words will never pass away."

or **1 Samuel 3:19 (NIV):** "And Samuel grew, and the LORD was with him, and did let none of his words fall to the ground." (I usually memorize scripture; it has been several years now so unsure which of the two it was).

Whichever verse it was, it gave me the confidence I needed to pray in faith for this couple despite their circumstances or my fatigue. Faith had also determined her years of infertility had ended. She locked her faith with mine and we signed the deal with God!

She and I fasted during the Christmas holidays, she in the UK and I in Holland. We decided she would visit me to seal our prayers of agreement and to see a doctor which we did. The results were nothing short of a miracle from God!

Faith was small in stature with ageless features therefore could have easily been mistaken for someone in her late thirties. The French doctor studied her demographics as well as her clinical information. After examining her, he bobbed his head comically up and down, peering at Faith then back at her report. Clearly, he appeared skeptical concerning her predicament due to her age and recommended to me in French to abort the baby (assuming it was a mistake).

I gestured to Faith to get dressed and we quickly thanked him rushing from the office laughing like two young teenagers. We located my car expediently, hopped inside locking the door behind us. We sat in silence for a moment before bursting into hysterical laughter remembering the doctor's facial expression of alarm, mouth agape as we hurried past him into the fresh, cool night air.

Although the sky was dark, the stars were visible twinkling to the melody of the trees which swayed in a dance to the fierce Northern wind. Everything about that evening seemed supernatural. Even time appeared to stand-still! Our hilarious laughter ceased abruptly. We became sober at the realization of the magnitude of the blessing Father had bestowed upon us. Faith pulled her coat tight across her small frame pressing her hand upon her flat tummy as we glorified God.

I prayed **Psalms 126:1 (NIV)** over her quite frequently after that: "When the LORD restored the fortunes of Zion (Faith}, we were like those who dreamed".   This resonated in her Spirit!

This dear sister stayed with my family often during her pregnancy. She had plans to return for her last trimester; however, we were packed and ready for our move to Malaysia by then! Dr Bero called to let me know she was in on our secret.
"Rhondy, take photos of Faith's stomach because people will never believe she has given birth after this many years of infertility," she wisely advised. I promised I would. I also made Dr. Bero vow she would not divulge our secret until after the appointed time. Not even my family knew the truth!

Nigeria has the greatest number of multiple births in the world nevertheless there is a stigmatism towards women who cannot conceive. I promptly took photos as proof of the pregnancy. Later when Faith returned to Nigeria with her baby girl, a huge celebration was given on their behalf! A beautiful Thanksgiving service was organized unto the Lord which I was unable to attend because of our family's relocation to Malaysia. I was told streets were sequestered as people danced and celebrated this wondrous blessing from the Lord!

"He settles the childless woman in her home as a happy mother of children." Praise the LORD. **Psalms 113:9 (NIV).**

In that glorious conference, the Lord accomplished something for this dear Saint as well as for me. My dream to move to Malaysia came to fruition which led to my involvement with Oasis Ladies Bible Study! The Lord has marvelous plans for us, Dear Ones.

For I know the plans I have for you," declares the Lord, "plans to prosper you and not to harm you, plans to give you hope and a future." **Jeremiah 29:11 (NIV).**

The Bible says further in **2 Corinthians 1:20 (NKJV) :**
"For all the promises of God in Him *are* Yes, and in Him Amen, to the glory of God through us."

Let us Pray:
Father, all your promises are Yes and Amen to the glory of God through us! We are like those who dreamed when you restored all our fortunes, oh Lord. There may be sisters reading this devotional who are seeking the fruit of the womb, dear Father, please grant their request. Others might have dreams yet to be fulfilled, make dreams come true, oh Lord. Thank you for listening to our prayers of supplication! In Jesus Mighty Name! Amen.

Song: Good, Good Father by Chris Tomlin

Day 37 – Spiritual Housecleaning

"But keep away from the devoted things, so that you will not bring about your own destruction by taking any of them. Otherwise you will make the camp of Israel liable to destruction and bring trouble on it." **Joshua 6:18 (NIV).**

While walking in the cool of the evening today, my husband reminded me of a time long ago when he was Director of the Bible Institute in Congo. His students were meeting at our home coincidently the same time I had an appointment with a young couple in our living room.

The woman was gorgeous with a chic hairstyle, her husband was handsome, they appeared to be upper class Congolese. I was certain their issue had to do with infertility therefore our prayer time would be short. I was correct on the first assumption but not the second!

In my usual custom, I prayed to ask the Lord for guidance during the meeting. No sooner than I lifted my voice, there was a demonic manifestation which lasted for the next 9 hours! My husband and his students meeting on the veranda were a Godsend as they were able to intercede throughout the entire episode.

Shortly after midnight, I whispered to my husband we needed to do Spiritual House Cleaning in her home before she would totally be free.

Spiritual housekeeping simply means removing the things in your home that have been devoted to the enemy or false gods. It could be a statue of Buddha, a Dream Catcher or a Zodiac book etc.

I should also mention an 'innocent visit' to a palm reader could also be a hindrance in your prayer life. Any of these items or if you are a participant in these activities give the enemy free access to your life and WILL not leave until proper Spiritual Housecleaning has been done. By having these things, you give Satan and his cohorts liberal entry into your home.

The Bible says "Or again, how can anyone enter a strong man's house and carry off his possessions unless he first ties up the strong man?

Then he can plunder his house." **Matthew 12:29 (NIV).** We needed to remove any objects or artifacts in her home associated with the enemy before she would be free. These items allowed a demonic doorway into her life which meant Satan had legal access to stay although we were praying for deliverance.

This necessitated that we go to her home in a two-car convoy to rid her home of "the strong man". Entering her home, she went straight to the devoted items and threw them outside, they exploded with a loud bang! It was during this event that my husband began to believe in the need for people to be delivered!

Joshua lost a battle which he could have easily won because of Achan who kept items devoted to the devil in his home.

This is what it says in **Joshua 7:10-12 (NIV)**:
"**10** The Lord said to Joshua, 'Stand up! What are you doing down on your face? **11** Israel has sinned; they have violated my covenant, which I commanded them to keep. They have taken some of the devoted things; they have stolen, they have lied, they have put them with their own possessions. **12** That is why the Israelite's cannot stand against their enemies'.

Because Achan had taken a beautiful robe, a bar of gold and silver coins from the Babylonians, the entire nation of Israel lost the battle, because of one man! Joshua took Achan, his family, animals virtually all he owned and stoned them to death until God's fury subsided!"

After 40 days of fasting and prayer, we have cleansed our spiritual temple but what about our physical home? You do not want to suffer the wrath of God and at worst have unanswered prayers due to disobedience. If after having made the sacrifice of walking with the Lord so closely and intimately over this period of time, you return to your brick and mortar home without doing spiritual housecleaning, you will experience Spiritual warfare till you rid your home of these devoted items.

Susanne, our Oasis founder was a collector of dragons notably those with the same name as her husband's. After one strange occurrence in her home, I warned her to get rid of those hideous artifacts, but she argued they were nothing, but expensive pieces of art placed in her home solely for the purpose of decoration. No power lay within them, later she found out she could not have been more mistaken.

Shortly afterwards, both she and her daughter started experiencing strange dreams involving tornadoes. The Holy Spirit told her these dreams were related to her collection of dragons. After a careful research she discovered the truth and finally decided to rid her home of the dragons and any other questionable statues or items indicated by the Lord.

After doing Spiritual Housecleaning her home felt squeaky clean and she nor her daughter had any other dreams of tornadoes. She began to grow and thrive in the Lord. Prior to that her spiritual growth seemed to be stunted but after her Spiritual Housecleaning took place she began to soar!

Do you need to do spiritual house cleaning before this fast ends? If you are not sure which items you need to dispose of, please feel free to contact me. Obedience is paramount in this situation.

Pray:
Heavenly Father, I build an altar in my home as I remove all the devoted items you have indicated to me have to go. I plead the blood of Jesus over my household. Forgive me Lord for my involvement in _____ I choose to obey you than to worry about the cost or sentimental value these items may hold. Do not remove your Covenant of Peace from us, Oh Lord.

By the same token, we ask for forgiveness on behalf of our Country and State, our President, governor and our mayor. We have despicable practices that do not honor You, Father, forgive us for we have sinned. In Jesus Mighty Name, Amen.

Day 38 – God's Great Commission – Release the Dove!

God is in control of our destinies. On every occasion we are in, He uses us to spread his sweet fragrance amongst others. " For we are to God the pleasing aroma of Christ among those who are being saved and those who are perishing." **2 Corinthians 2:15 (NIV)**.

What a mighty God we serve who begins a new story with us in the fire when we are yielded to Him! Fire purifies and once the goldsmith sees his image in it, he knows the masterpiece is ready! When our Heavenly Father, The Goldsmith snatches us out of the fire at his designated time we are ready to be used by Him. He is an on-time God, never too late!

Remember the story of Shadrach, Meshach, and Abednego who were thrown into the fiery furnace by the King in **Daniel 3:22-25 (NIV)**?

"**22** Because the king's order was urgent and the furnace overheated, the flame of the fire killed those men who took up Shadrach, Meshach, and Abednego. **23** And these three men, Shadrach, Meshach, and Abednego, fell bound into the burning fiery furnace. **24** Then King Nebuchadnezzar was astonished and rose up in haste. He declared to his counselors, 'Did we not cast three men bound into the fire?' They answered and said to the king, 'True, O king.' **25** He answered and said, 'But I see four men unbound, walking in the midst of the fire, and they are not hurt; and the appearance of the fourth is like a son of the gods'."

Hallelujah, Jesus got in the fiery furnace with them! They were not burned and there was NO smell of smoke! In addition, they were no longer bound! Today you may feel like you are bound by your past, by alcohol, porn, drugs, food whatever additions might have bound you, The King of glory can get in your fiery furnace and loose you today, praise the Lord!

When we are a spiritual firebrand, people take notice!

Acts 5:15 (NIV): "As a result, people brought the sick into the streets and laid them on beds and mats so that at least Peter's shadow might fall on some of them as he passed by."

Acts 19:12 (NIV): "so that even handkerchiefs and aprons that had touched him were taken to the sick, and their illnesses were cured, and the evil spirits left them." (Speaking of Paul).

2 Kings 13:21 (NIV): "Once while some Israelites' were burying a man, suddenly they saw a band of raiders; so, they threw the man's body into Elisha's tomb. When the body touched Elisha's bones, the man came to life and stood up on his feet."

Mark 16:17-18 (KJV):
"**17** And these signs shall follow them that believe; In my name shall they cast out devils; they shall speak with new tongues. **18** They shall take up serpents; and if they drink any deadly thing, it shall not hurt them; they shall lay hands on the sick, and they shall recover."
These are all powerful scriptures that teach us that Jesus Heals! He uses the foolish things to confound the wise! An apron, a handkerchief, a shadow and our hands. But what's the common

denominator? Yes, Jesus was in each of these situations as part of the Trinity. The Holy Spirit was present and working with them.

Acts 10:38
"How God anointed Jesus of Nazareth with the Holy Spirit and power, and how he went around doing good and healing all who were under the power of the devil, because God was with him."

The Great Commission was given to us as believers. We need to go into all the world and preach the gospel. In today's age, many have begun to preach via television, YouTube and many GO as missionaries to various countries devoting their lives to this kind of work. We have incredibly good Missionary friends Janice and Gary Dickinson who did Missionary work in Congo for almost 30 years and are currently breaking ground in Gabon. They have devoted their lives for the cause of Jesus Christ!

But often, the Lord simply uses us in our current circumstances to be light and salt to others around us in our sphere of influence. He has given us the Great Commission as our mandate, and He has promised to be with us. In addition, he has given us the Holy Spirit! What more could we ask for?

Matthew 28:16-20 (NIV):
"The Great Commission"
16 Then the eleven disciples went to Galilee, to the mountain where Jesus had told them to go. **17** When they saw him, they worshiped him; but some doubted. **18** Then Jesus came to them and said, "All authority in heaven and on earth has been given to me. **19** Therefore go and make disciples of all nations, baptizing them in the name of the Father and of the Son and of the Holy Spirit, **20** and teaching them to obey everything I have commanded you. And surely, I am with you always, to the very end of the age."

Let us pray:

"Our Father, our faith remains rooted and grounded in your Word and not just historical things. Although it is integrally related to life we pray that our own faith may grow strong and be powerful as we see the despair around us, the shaking of foundations, the changing of that which has long been taken to be permanent, the overthrowing of empires and the rising of others. Abba, our eyes are steadfast on you as our Unchanging Omnipresent God. The One Whose Word is Eternal. As the Lord Jesus himself said, "Heaven and earth shall pass away, but my Word shall never pass away." Matthew 24:35 (Lift up your hands as a sign of surrender unto God).

Use me, oh Lord in this latter day to become a catalyst for change. In my sphere of influence, enable me to Release the Dove and see miraculous occurrences take place. I pray in Jesus Mighty name, Amen.

If you prayed that prayer with a sincere heart, get ready for a supernatural manifestation to take place!

Day 39 – The Lord is MY Shepherd – A Tribute to Rose

Hebrews 11: 39 has provided me with a source of victory for many years. It has enabled me to stay the course when it seemed as if I should have given up. I refer to Hebrews 11 as the "Hall of Faith" yet **verses 39-40** at first glance appear to be a contradiction to faith, but they are not. They are in effect the accomplishment of it!

"**39** These were all commended for their faith, yet none of them received what had been promised, **40** since God had planned something better for us so that only together with us would they be made perfect."

My husband and his colleague from the University in Congo were blessed to be recipients of a scholarship to attend University in the USA. Both studied Finance but in different cities. I had had the privilege of getting to know Rose in the States and later was welcomed into her family's home in Congo. Her twin sister was a doctor and became remarkably close to me.

Rose married a wonderful man in the USA, had two beautiful children and resided in NY. We all tried to stay in touch, but communication was difficult in those days. It was a shock to find out later Rose had breast cancer and had passed away. She chose to carry her secret to her grave, not seeking care, rather trusting the Lord with the ultimate cure.

I often wondered why she did not choose treatment. She and my husband were the top two students at their university and therefore considered the cream of the crop in the higher echelon of intelligence. Both were highly successful at completing their MBA studies in the USA. The decision Rose made was to trust the Lord wholeheartedly and to lean not on her own understanding but in all her ways, acknowledge him and He would direct her path (**Proverbs 3:5**).

Many may argue at the seemingly stupidity of her decision, but I do not. Who are we to judge? It was ultimately hers to make and her faith superseded anything doctors could offer. We may never know the truth. Perhaps she was already at Stage 4 once diagnosed and chose quality of life in order to remain a good Mom to her young children, but that is not the point I want to make here. Rose stood in faith despite her afflicted body by saying with her actions, "Lord if you don't heal me, you will take me home." She was a great woman of faith!

We will all ultimately have to travel that road one day. David wrote one of the most famous Psalms in the Bible which is a great source of hope and comfort to those who travel down the windy path of LIFE to Eternal LIFE.

Let's read **Psalm 23 (MSG)** :
"1-3 God, my shepherd! I don't need a thing. You have bedded me down in lush meadows, you find me quiet pools to drink from. True to your word, you let me catch my breath
and send me in the right direction.**4** Even when the way goes through Death Valley, I'm not afraid when you walk at my side. Your trusty shepherd's crook makes me feel secure. **5** You serve me a six-course dinner right in front of my enemies. You revive my drooping head; my cup brims with blessing. **6** Your beauty and love chase after me
every day of my life. I'm back home in the house of God
for the rest of my life. "

"How frail is humanity! How short is life, how full of trouble!" Job exclaimed. **Job 14:1 (NLT)**.

Pray:
Lord, at the end of my life, I do not seek to gather my trophies as the Pharaohs of old did wishing to take them along at the end of life's journey. Instead, my most valuable treasures are my family and loved ones, those are the ones I would like to have surrounding my bed during those final moments before breathing my last breath. Psalm 23 provides hope to each of us knowing you are our Shepherd accompanying us along the way. Verse 6 says in the NIV, "Goodness and Mercy" shall follow me. Your goodness, mercy, love and kindness are better than life!

Psalm 63:3 (NIV) declares:
"Because your love is better than life, my lips will glorify you."

"You have conquered death, my God." Your Word declares in **1 Corinthians 15:55-56 (NIV):**
"**55** "'Where, O death, is your victory? Where, O death, is your sting?' **56** The sting of death is sin, and the power of sin is the law. **57** But thanks be to God! He gives us the victory through our Lord Jesus Christ."

Because you are my Savior, I have given my life to you back in 1984 (insert your date and circumstance) when I knelt on the floor of my apartment on campus. I know Lord that my transition from earth to heaven will be like a blink of an eye. Just knowing you will be with me every step of the way makes all the difference to me. Thank you, Father, in Jesus Name Amen.

Day 40 – Our Unchanging God

What a joy and a privilege to have journeyed with you during this 40-day devotional. In retrospect, we did not commence this journey envisioning all that we have encountered, did we? The landscape and tapestry have changed drastically over the past few weeks destabilizing our worlds.

Most of us were simply concerned about trivialities such as what kind of fast we would undertake. None of us would have imagined the chaos the world has endeared during these 40 days and beyond.

Yet and still, those of us who have kept our eyes upon the Lord are in perfect peace. The Israelites leaving Egypt for freedom did not expect to cross the Red Sea or sojourn in the desert for 40 years. It

was a bittersweet experience. Yet when Caleb emerged from the wilderness, he declared in **Joshua 14 (NIV):**
"**7** I was forty years old when Moses the servant of the Lord sent me from Kadesh Barnea to explore the land. And I brought him back a report according to my convictions, **8** but my fellow Israelites who went up with me made the hearts of the people melt in fear. I, however, followed the Lord my God wholeheartedly. **9** So on that day Moses swore to me, 'The land on which your feet have walked will be your inheritance and that of your children forever, because you have followed the Lord my God wholeheartedly.'
11b-12a – 'So here I am today, eighty-five years old! **11** I am still as strong today as the day Moses sent me out; I'm just as vigorous to go out to battle now as I was then. **12** Now give me this hill country that the Lord promised me that day.'"

Dearly beloved, the promises of the Lord have not changed from when we commenced this 40-day fast! His Covenant of peace still follows you and your posterity. Caleb chose not to see the giants in the land but preferred to see God's promises. Whose report will you believe when the world seems to be crumbling around you. Caleb chose to believe the Word of the Lord. He gave a report according to his convictions. Whereby the other spies saw giants and destruction, Caleb and Joshua saw the Promised Land!

Galatians 6:9 (NIV) gives us renewed focus with this Word:
"**9** Let us not become weary in doing good, for at the proper time we will reap a harvest if we do not give up. "

Like Caleb, have you followed your God wholeheartedly or has your heart melted like the other spies who accompanied Caleb and Joshua and were afraid of the giants? They forgot all about their Great God. They forgot about how he had brought them out of Egypt with his mighty outstretched arm and divided the Red Sea for them to cross!

They looked upon the giants and lost all confidence in God's promises.

Beloved, have you done the same by averting your eyes from our great immutable God who put the stars in the sky and who created Heaven and earth?

Job 38:4-7 (NIV) reads:
"**4** Where were you when I laid the earth's foundation? Tell me, if you understand. **5** Who marked off its dimensions? Surely you know! Who stretched a measuring line across it?
6 On what were its footings set, or who laid its cornerstone—**7** while the morning stars sang together and all the angels shouted for joy?"

Oh, He is indeed worthy to be praised!

Psalms 113:3-6 (NIV) proclaims:
"**3** From the rising of the sun to the place where it sets, the name of the Lord is to be praised. **4** The Lord is exalted over all the nations, his glory above the heavens. **5** Who is like the Lord our God, the One who sits enthroned on high, **6** who stoops down to look on the heavens and the earth?

Release Community, Psalms 34:3d declares:
"**3** O magnify the Lord with me and let us exalt his name together".

I exhort you to be steadfast and unmovable in what you know to be the Love of Christ.
"Every good gift and every perfect gift is from above, coming down from the Father of lights, with whom there is no variation or shadow due to change." **James 1:17 (NIV)**

The World may appear to be changing before your very eyes. But you can rest assured in knowing our God does not change. He is and will be the most stable in your life from here going into eternity.

Wherever this life may take you, even if your circumstances change for better or for worse, remember in whom you have believed. Your world may Change but God never changes.

"Jesus Christ is the same yesterday and today and forever." **Hebrews 13:8 (NIV)**.
His love is from everlasting to everlasting. Repeat with me the following verses of scripture:

Romans 8:38-39 (NLT):
"**38** And I am convinced that nothing can ever separate us from God's love. Neither death nor life, neither angels nor demons neither our fears for today nor our worries about tomorrow—not even the powers of hell can separate us from God's love. **39** No power in the sky above or in the earth below—indeed, nothing in all creation will ever be able to separate us from the love of God that is revealed in Christ Jesus our Lord."

Passion – In Christ Alone

https://youtu.be/7kmPZywtN4Y

Editor's Note – Afterword | Katherine Voorvelt

Rhonda asked me to edit her 'Release the Dove 40-day fast devotional '. It was a pleasure for me to say yes as it was an opportunity to bless Rhonda a little as she has been such a generous and loving 'blesser' in my life. Little did I know that this task would again be more of a blessing to me than my editing was to her.

I had heard of her 'Release the Dove' Study but had not been part of it and had read a few of the devotionals but not fasted. I opened the Draft to Day 1 and there it was – a rich, life-changing, powerful and riveting devotion for the day. I forgot that I was meant to be editing and basically consumed the Word and message for the day. A Michelin Star meal had been served to me. I prayed the prayer indicated at the end of the devotion earnestly and then remembered that I should be editing! I was doubly blessed as I went back to the beginning and started doing so, each word and scripture slow and sure, and found myself praying that I was rich soil so that the seeds being planted would grow and be strong in me.

Each of the 40 devotions proved to be made with fresh ingredients right from the food-store of the Holy Spirit and I was hungry for such wholesome food. Needless to say, it took me ages to complete the editing task!

Apart from the Word, Wisdom and Prayers, this Devotional is somewhat biographical. The reader gets to know bit of the life and times of Rhonda Dikoko, her family and friends. What a lifetime of challenges, victories, and journeys both geographic and spiritual. Certainly, enough to make me dizzy! It reveals Rhonda as I know her to be. A woman with seemingly endless energy and great faith, who puts Father God, Christ Jesus and the Holy Spirit first in all things. A strong woman released to be all that God intended her to be. Just like you and me!

Note from the author:
Mary (L) and Katherine (R) are my Covenant Sisters in The Hague. When I left Holland to move back to the States in Dec 2018, this rainbow appeared outside my window as I sat in the lounge awaiting my flight to take off. In my Release Bible Study, I spoke of how the rainbow appeared on my wedding photo miraculously in 1986 and usually shows up as a sign in major cross-roads in my life. Here a double rainbow appeared!

Endorsement | Mary Thomas

On a cold blustery Sunday morning in January 2017, it was the first time my family and I stepped into the foyer of the Redeemer International Church of The Hague. We were met by a vivacious colorful woman who welcomed us and introduced herself by saying, "Good morning! My name is Rhonda, just like the song "Help Me Rhonda," now you'll never forget!" And she was right, how could we forget? We were from America and very familiar with this popular Beach Boys' song. But besides that, we will never forget this warm welcome and who could guess that this woman would become one of my closest sisters in the Lord – a covenant sister. Rhonda Dikoko is a whirlwind, a dynamo, a beautiful, passionate and committed woman of God. I know of her toil in the Lord, how she gives 100% in everything she does. I've personally experienced this love and compassion at time when I was sick at home for a few weeks. Even though she was working full time, she came almost every day; to check on me, to bring me homemade soup and to give her encouragement. She doesn't know it, but she carried me those weeks and I will never forget the blessing she was to me and my family.

As you read this devotional book, you will see a glimpse of the wonderful woman Rhonda is, but I know with all her heart – she would want you to not see her, but Jesus Christ in her, daily working in her to bring the full glory unto God.

- - - -

Mary Thomas, member of Redeemer International Church of The Hague.

www.ingramcontent.com/pod-product-compliance
Ingram Content Group UK Ltd.
Pitfield, Milton Keynes, MK11 3LW, UK
UKHW021838220326
11410UKWH00011B/97